The Four Stone Tree

The Four Stone Tree

by

VINCENT BYRNE

Published in 2003 by
Vincent Byrne, No 1 The Close, Oldtown Mill, Celbridge, Co. Kildare, Ireland,
in conjunction with Blessington Family & Local History Group.

ISBN 0 9546248 0 7
A CIP Catalogue record for this book is available from the British Library.

The following are acknowledged as sources of information for this book.

The National Library of Ireland
The Courier Newspaper
The Freeman's Journal
Saunders News Letter
Dublin Evening Post
Faulkner's Dublin Journal
The Leinster Leader
The Wicklow People
The Wicklow Newsletter
Public Records Office NI
Kildare Co. Library
Wicklow Co. Library

Photographs by kind permission of:
Hulton Getty Archives
The Irish Times
Sportsfile
National Photographic Archives
National Library of Ireland
PRONI
Pat Hanlon
Aidan Cruise
The Byrne Scrapbook
Paddy Magee
Jannett Halligan

1798 prints courtesy Kildare Co. Library.

The assistance of Fintan Byrne, who gave many hours of his time in compiling this book is also acknowledged.

This book is grant aided by Wicklow Rural Partnership Ltd., The Minister for the Department of Community, Rural & Gaeltacht Affairs and the EU Commission under the Leader+ Programme.

PRINTED BY THE LEINSTER LEADER, NAAS, CO. KILDARE.

Contents

Dedicated to the memory of my parents
TOMMY & MOLLY BYRNE
and all the people mentioned in this book who made
Blessington's history.

The Four Stone Tree

The Four Stone Tree has stood in the centre of Blessington since it was a sapling, when planted the late 17th Century. It has been a silent witness to the creation of the town, to its trials and tribulations, its conflicts and celebration of achievements all down the years.

This symbol of "citizenship" of an historic creation has a special place in the hearts and minds of the inhabitants. It is regarded as the birthright of the natives whose ancestors were part of the evolution and enthusiastically adapted by the new residents who chose to set up home in the area.

Originally the centre of a magnificent landscaped square at the entrance to the Blessington Demesne, the surrounding area was blighted by reckless bad planning decisions by the council. The erection of public toilets, a loading bank and flowerbeds in a most inappropriate location in the 1950's and in controversial circumstances served to alter the original grandeur of the square. It was the dominant position and splendour of **The Four Stone Tree** that protected the character of the town in the face of adversity. It has been the bulwark against planning vandalism and will continue to be so in the future with the support of the residents.

The traditions and fond memories that this edifice evokes has inspired the title for this book.

Blessington

WHILE the area known as Blessington existed since God made the world, it is its relative recent history in which we have an interest. Ireland was not always an island. During the ice age the land mass that now constitutes the island was attached to the landmass of continental Europe. About 20,000 years ago the ice age came to an end, the ice melted, water levels rose, the lowlands were submerged providing a water barrier between Ireland and Britain, and between Britain and the continent thereby forming two separate islands. That was about 18,000 BC.

When the ice glaciers melted they gouged out the mountains, the valleys and the riverbeds including the Liffey valley and the area around Blessington. The meltdown left a flooded area from Brittas, through Blessington and extended down to Hollywood. When this flood receded it left in its wake the sand and gravel deposits that now constitutes Blessington sandpits. Throughout the ages we were visited by various invaders. Some were peaceful, some were warlike, some were conquerors and some were defenders. About 10,000 years ago the first inhabitants started to appear in Ireland. Initially they settled in the northern part of the country in the river areas and percolated south to the river Boyne, the Liffey and the Slaney.

Wicklow shows signs of habitation about 7,000 BC, but Blessington shows evidence of habitation about 2,000 BC. Artifacts unearthed in Blessington from this period are on display in the British museum. In the national museum in Dublin a reconstructed cist grave is on display containing an encrusted burial urn containing a cremated remains. Alongside was a vase food vessel. These were unearthed at Burgage and were dated back to the same period. It was the arrival of Celts and the invasions by the Vikings in the tenth century, and the invasion of the Normans in the twelfth century that left their mark on our present culture. It was the Celts that influenced the development of our language and culture, while the Vikings established the foundations of our capital city and other ports. The visible contribution of our Norman visitors is their legacy of Norman castles throughout the land. The era of High Kings, Kings and chieftains was followed by the plantation of our country by British invaders. This in turn led to the period of protestant ascendancy during which Blessington came into being.

Blessington in 1900

Blessington Upper end of Main Street

Main Street, Blessington.

Main Street, Blessington.

Plantation

BRITISH rule was established in Ireland with the defeat of some Irish chieftains and with the collusion of others. The clans of Wicklow were the O'Byrnes and the O'Tooles. The O'Byrne clan date back to the twelfth century. They were originally masters in Kildare but were dislodged and retreated to the Wicklow Mountains where they established themselves as a formidable force. On many occasions they proved themselves to be the ultimate hill fighters.

Dominant British forces confiscated the land as the spoils of war and redistributed it as a reward to their own warlords. It was during this transition that the town of Blessington, as we know it, was established in 1669. This development had its geneses in the act of settlement of 1668, passed by the British parliament. Under charter from King Charles 11 of England, archbishop Michael Boyle acquired 410 acres of forfeited land on which he proceeded to develop the borough and corporation of Blessington.

Blessington was to be administered by archbishop Boyle as Sovereign and two bailiffs. He was also chancellor of all Ireland making him a very important and influential figure in the country. He built a mansion on his newly acquired land four years later. As part of the ongoing development he built the Protestant church in 1683, which survives to the present day as a working church and is the surviving monument to his reign. In addition to his demesne, he was also awarded approximately 14,000 acres of adjoining land to make him one of the biggest landowners in the country. Blessington and the Boyle lands were in the barony of Talbotstown, which sent two members to the British Parliament. These members were not elected but were nominated by the landowners.

Archbishop Boyle performed his spiritual and political duties from his mansion in Blessington for thirty-three years. He lived to the ripe old age of ninety-three years, died in 1702,and was the last ecclesiastical Lord Chancellor of Ireland. The Blessington property was inherited by his son, the Earl of Blessington, then his daughter, and then passed to Arthur Hill, later to become the Marquis of Downshire, whose estate was in Hillsborough.

Under the new owner the mansion was used as a hunting lodge and the lands were a source of a significant rental income. He was regarded by his tenants as a good and fair landlord and left the day to day running of the estate to his estate manager.

Other large landowners in the area were, the Hornidges in Tulfaris, the Smiths in Baltyboys, the Earl of Milltown in Russborough, the Finnmores in Ballyward and the Moores in Manor Kilbride.

Lord Downshire did not take a great interest in Blessington but he was relieved of the responsibility for the mansion when the rebel soldiers of the 1798 rebellion burned it to the ground. The mansion was not rebuilt and over subsequent years the stonework was removed and put to other uses. A small portion of the wine cellar remains. Only occasionally did he visit the estate and stayed in the administration building beside the church which now operates as a hotel.

Archbishop of Dublin Michael Boyle
(1609-1702)
Established town of Blessington, 1669.

Arthur Hill
(1753-1801)
2nd Marquis of Downshire)

Conflict

THE population of Blessington at the beginning of the twenty first century stands at about 2,600 people. Very few of the residents realise that the street on which they walk, at different stages of history reverberated to the sound of horse cavalry, yeomanry, gunfire and armoured cars. The town played a part in three major conflicts in the course of Irish history. They were the 1798 rebellion, the war of independence, and the civil war in addition to a famine. Prior to these events there were the usual skirmishes between the chieftains and the local constabulary.

The first recorded instance of loss of life in such confrontational circumstances occurred in 1538 and was recorded in the papers of Henry viii. The constable of Rathmore, John Kelway, had executed two members of the O'Toole clan for poaching. O'Toole demanded an explanation for the drastic action and a meeting was arranged at Three Castles in Blessington. Neither side displayed any trust and in the inevitable confrontation Kelway was killed. In the altercation Kelway's men killed a local farmer and his labourers by setting fire to their thatched farmhouse. It is reported that up to sixty householders were killed by Kelway's men.

The 1798 rebellion was a landmark occurrence in the course of Irish history. While the rebellion was put down, it served as a signpost and inspiration to a future generation in the constant quest for Irish freedom from imperial domination. The area of Wexford and south Wicklow was the cockpit of the military action during this period, but the hostilities extended to West Wicklow and Blessington has its own historic involvement. Blackamore Hill overlooking Blessington, and situated at the back of Knockierin, was the site of a major rebel camp. The prominent rebel leader General Joe Holt, himself a Wicklow man and a protestant, used the camp extensively and exerted his influence over the area.

A division of yeomanry controlled by the local estate owners based in Blessington served to defend the British ethos as represented by the landed gentry and maintain their wealth. The yeomanry were based in St. Mary's church and used the church spire as a defensive position.

While the United Irishmen were formed in 1791, the plans for a rebellion came to fruition at the beginning of 1798. However, the town of

Blessington was to get a taste of the violent nature of the rebellion to come when, in August of 1797, a rebel force converged on the town, armed with Firelocks (Guns) and Pikes, in search of an informer, who was in the protective custody of the Blessington Yeomanry. He had betrayed several leaders of the United Irishmen and was about to suffer the consequences of his actions.

The Yeomanry were heavily outnumbered by the Rebels and were forced to relinquish their prisoner to his accusers. A report in the Faulkner's Dublin Journal stated that "he was dragged from the arms of his family, alleging he was an informer, and was murdered in a cruel manner, which only the diabolical ingenuity of the United Irishmen could devise, severing the head from the body and tearing the limbs apart".

The same fate befell a Walter Read who was executed on Blackamore Hill for a similar offence. He was executed by a method known as gibbiting.

At the same time the Militia were carrying out executions in Ireland by means of portable gallows and by "Pitch Capping". This was the practice of fitting a cap of a mixture of tar and gunpowder on their victims head and setting it alight. A militia officer by the name of Captain Hempenstall was known as the "Walking Gallows". He was a very tall broad shouldered individual who having tied the noose around his victim's neck, hauled the rope over his shoulder and dangled him on his back until dead.

These methods and occurrences are well documented in accounts of the conflict published during this period.

Another execution was that of Jonathan Eves, who was living in Baltyboys. Joe Holt's troops, on their way from Hollywood to Blessington, picked up Eves on suspicion of informing. He was shot down by Henry Downes at the camp before Holt had an opportunity to give him a fair trial. During the raid on the Downshire Demesne, a defender was also killed by another of Holt's men, which he claimed was in self defence.

Many other incidents of a confrontational nature took place in the town. One such incident is recorded in Joe Holt's own memoirs. Holt fed and sustained his men by accepting the hospitality of sympathetic supporters, by commandeering supplies and by rustling cattle from the estate owners.

It was on a rustling mission that Holt's band of rebels visited Blessington at the beginning of September 1798. The object of his attention was a herd of cattle in Downshire's demesne. Blessington was heavily fortified by the yeomanry and they had a gun placement on the spire of the church. A section of Holt's men surrounded the church and pinned down the yeomanry with heavy fire while the remainder herded cattle, sheep, and horses from the demesne. The Rev. Hill Benson, rector of the church at the time, lost his fine horse in the same raid. One of Holt's men was shot dead on the street, as was the yeoman who fired the fatal shot.

Later that same month Blessington was to be the centre of military activity for a second time. A force of about 2000 soldiers from Dublin marched on Blessington and met up with a contingent of cavalry already based in the town. They assembled their force in Toopers Field in close proximity to the village where General Lake had his headquarters. This area is still known by that name to the present day as a result of the military activity during this period. The force left Blessington in pursuit of the insurgents, raided Blackamore hill without success as the camp had been evacuated, then checking their usual haunts, they eventually discovered Holt's troops on Cloone hill near Arklow. They surrounded them and settled down for the night with a view to mounting an assault next morning. At sunrise they discovered that Holt's men had breached the cordon under cover of darkness and had disappeared without trace.

The rebellion ended in the autumn of 1798 with the defeat of the United Irishmen and Blessington returned to the daily grind of the tenant/landlord relationship. Two years later the Irish Parliament voted itself out of existence with the act of union of 1800. The local representatives of Talbotstown lost their seats, their power and influence but were induced to commit this deed of abject surrender for a bribe of 15,000. Ireland had become integrated within the United Kingdom, an act that The British parliament would live to regret.

Joseph Holt (1756-1826) General of the Irish Rebels in 1798.

Top: Mansion burning by the Rebels in 1798.

Left: Pitch Capping Execution by the British Militia in 1798.

[Etchings by George Cruckshank in 1845]

Famine – Conflict With Nature

THE tenant/landlord relationship came into sharp Focus in the 1840 period. In the rural areas the tenants were surviving in extremely poor circumstances and lived in poverty. Their crops were used to pay rents to the estate owners in return for use of the land and for the hovels in which they lived. The potato crop was retained to feed families. That relationship was tested to the full when the potato crop failed as a result of the dreaded blight.

Blessington and surrounding area was not as badly affected as the rest of rural Ireland. In general the local estate owners were very good landlords who made a genuine effort to alleviate the hardship. Some of the Estate owners were in strained financial circumstances themselves but the Marquis of Downshire was a very wealthy man. The estate owners availed of relief grants to undertake land drainage and road building schemes, thereby employing the local peasantry. In addition to Blessington, Lord Downshire owned estates in Kilkenny, Edenderry, Newry, Hillsborough, and England. It was acknowledged that he was one of the biggest landowners in the kingdom.

During this period Downshire built a Medical Dispensary on the Kilbride road in Blessington. The doctor was George Robinson who looked after the medical needs of the famine victims. It soon emerged that, due to weakness from hunger, the victims were developing a fever. To combat the problem Blessington Fever Hospital was built. It was situated on the edge of the village on the junction of the Kilmalum road and the Naas road. It was opened in 1845 and was extensively used for the duration of the famine. Many of the victims died, some went to the poorhouses in Naas and Baltinglass, while other families emigrated to America on assisted passages, financed by their landlords. The cost of building the Blessington hospital was subscribed to by The Hornidge, Smith, Finnmore and Downshire estates, in addition to Doctor Robinson.

The ruins of the Famine Village which existed at Cloughclea in the 1850s.

Second Military Conflict

IN the years between 1919 and 1922 the street of Blessington was once again to become the scene of military confrontation. Just 124 years after the activities of the United Irishmen in the village, arms were once more used against the same foe, the British army.

On Monday 24th April 1916 Patrick Pearse and his men marched into the GPO in Dublin and declared an Irish Republic. They were confronted by British forces but they resisted. Other strategic locations around the city were also occupied by the rebels who also came under attack. The hostilities lasted for five days, the rebels being forced to surrender under the superior heavy firepower of their adversaries. They were arrested and the signatories of the Proclamation were executed. The revolution only happened in Dublin and had not got the support of the Citizens of the city who cheered the British army for suppressing the troublemakers. When news of the executions got out there was a massive change in public opinion, which now supported the cause of the insurgents. The war of independence had begun.

Local participant in the 1916 rebellion was Paddy Kavanagh of Rathballylong, Blessington. He fought in Jacobs Factory in Bishop Street in Dublin during Easter Week, was arrested and interned in the UK prisons of Knutsford and Frangoch. On his release, he joined the Blessington unit of the South Dublin Brigade IRA and subsequently, organised a unit in Valleymount.

Volunteer units were organized in every village, town and townland in Ireland. Blessington was no exception. An active service unit, or flying column as they were sometimes called, was organized. They were originally attached to the Kildare brigade but were subsequently transferred to the 7th battalion of the South Dublin Brigade. By design, they were a small cohesive unit and proved to be very effective. Among the members of the active service unit based in Blessington were, Tommy Byrne, Quartermaster, Carbury Murphy, Bill Hanlon and Isaac Hamilton, all from Blessington, Tom Watkins, commanding officer, from Saggart, Paddy Farrell from Baltyboys, and Jimmy Hall from Brittas.

Tommy Byrne was born on 7th September 1894 in Ballintubber, Hollywood. He left school at 14 years of age and went to serve his time to the grocery trade in Cunninghams of Dunlavin. Having learned his trade he then purchased the lease of a three storey premises in Blessington at the end of 1919 from James Wallace for the sum of £2200, plus a yearly rent of £30. The premises had been operating as a grocery shop and public house. Tommy Byrne continued on this trade until the introduction of The Black and Tans who commandeered the premises and billeted their troops there. (This premises is now owned by the Dempsey family.)

The Royal Irish Constabulary was the British law enforcer in Ireland. They had their barracks in every village and were the eyes and ears of the British Establishment. The barracks in Blessington was located in the premises where the National School now stands. RIC Officers who occupied the station were Sgt. Patrick O'Hara and John McGowran. The strategy of the rebels was to harass the policemen, isolate them, attack them, force them to vacate the barracks, and then burn the station to the ground. Blessington barracks received this treatment, in March of 1920. It was closed down due to the Attention given to it by the local rebel force. In the British House of Commons one of the ministers responsible for Irish affairs stated in reply to a question that the Royal Irish Constabulary barracks in Blessington had been closed, the police service had been withdrawn and he was unable to say when it would be possible to reopen it. The routing of the Royal Irish Constabulary was a strategy which was successfully achieved. They were banished from Blessington. They retreated to Hollywood and subsequently to Naas.

At the same time Ballymore Eustace was also cleared of their presence, as was Dunlavin and Baltinglass. The IRA units were in control of West Wicklow. They patrolled the streets and set up the Sinn Fein courts. After the 1918 election success came the consolidation of The Sinn Fein vote all over Ireland. In the June 1920 local election. successful candidates in the Blessington District elections were, Peter P. O'Reilly, labour, Thomas Byrne, Sinn Fein, Michael Cullen, Sinn Fein. Lar Moore, Labour, Robert Shannon, Sinn Fein, John Murphy, Sinn Fein, William McGrath, Labour.

On June 23rd 1921, Blessington Court House and Lord Downshire's estate office were burned. All court books and estate papers, including title deeds to the houses in the town and Lord Downshire's rent records were piled up on the street and burned. The flames were still blazing at noon the following day. By coincidence a meeting of Blessington Town Tenants League was being held In the Band Hall on the next day. Mr. O'Connor, solicitor, advised the attendance that complications had arisen with the paperwork and the valuation process could not proceed for the present. The meeting was immediately adjourned.

The British Establishment in Dublin Castle lost their control, spying capability and resorted to introducing the dreaded Black and Tans. Britain was involved in their conflict in Europe, which stretched their regular army resources. In order to maintain their control in Ireland, they formed the Black and Tan force, recruiting army rejects, prison inmates and retired army personnel. Uniforms were in short supply so they dressed them in whatever was available. Their members wore black tunics and brown trousers, while others wore brown tunics and black trousers. They were a disparate lot and a ruthless bunch who were given a free hand to suppress the natives. They landed in Ireland on the 25th of March and were immediately in combat with the IRA. Throughout the following months many attacks were made on them by the Blessington active service unit.

The local RIC barracks, which had remained idle since its evacuation in March, was to receive special attention. Early in July the barracks was set on fire. It was not completely destroyed but was revisited a week later. On the first occasion the roof and part of the interior survived. The second effort was more successful, leaving only the walls standing. This action was taken in order to deny the use of the building to the Black and Tans. Petrol was commandeered in the village. No threats were made against the inhabitants and no attempt was made to terrorize them. The discharge of firearms into the air was an act of triumphalism as the flames engulfed the shell of the building.

There was no monthly petty sessions held in the courthouse in July. The volunteers were keeping law and order, ensuring that licensed premises closed at a reasonable hour. The nearest RIC station was at Hollywood. The IRA established their own courts and boycotted the British administered system of justice. The social activities of the village were organized by Cumann na Mbhan with a successful, well attended feis taking place in early August, using local artists. This activity was pursued in order to demonstrate that normal social activity would be enjoyed in spite of the presence of the 'Tans'. Many ambushes on the 'Tans' took place in Blessington, Kilbride, Brittas and Baltyboys. Arrests continued and were made under the Defence of the Realm Act, otherwise known as 'Dora'. During one of these ambushes in Blessington two of the active service unit were arrested and brought before the British military court and incarcerated in Mountjoy Jail. The prisoners were Isaac Hamilton and, the leader of the unit, Tommy Byrne.

On August 21st a large crowd gathered at the Blessington Steam Tram station to welcome home Isaac Hamilton, who had been released from jail. The Blessington fife and drum band also turned out for the occasion playing stirring airs. The assembled crowd formed up behind the band, with Mr. Hamilton hoisted shoulder high and marched to his home. The parade was headed by banners and tri colours. The crowd were urged not to forget Tommy Byrne who was still in jail. He was arrested at the same time as Mr. Hamilton.

The republican prisoners were being treated as criminals and were required to wear prison uniforms. They refused and went on hunger strike to press their case. Tommy Byrne joined the protest and spent 23 days on hunger strike. The strike ended when the prisoners were granted Prisoner of War status. Many of them were released because they were in poor condition and the plan was to rearrest them when returned to full health.

Scenes of great enthusiasm were witnessed when Tommy Byrne arrived from Mountjoy on his release. Three taxies in which he travelled with his Sinn Fein friends from Dublin were halted outside the town, at Cross Chapel, where a huge crowd had formed a procession. About 2000 people took part. Headed by the local fife and drum band, the torchlight procession marched through the town. The windows on each side of the street were illuminated. The Sinn Fein flags were very much in evidence and a banner with the words 'Cead Mile Failte from the people' was displayed. Mr Byrne was entertained in Murphy' s hotel (now West Wicklow House) where toasts were proposed and responded to. The night's Celebrations were wound up at an enjoyable dance in the Band Hall. The occasion was also marked by several bonfires which blazed on the surrounding heights, one being as far distant as the Embankment in Tallaght.

Demonstrations like this were numerous throughout Ireland and served to demonstrate widespread support for the Republican cause. Both prisoners returned to their unit and continued to harass the 'Tans' until the truce with the British government was declared. As all this local activity was taking place, the national movement under leaders such as Michael Collins, Harry Boland, Tom Barry, Ernie 0'Malley and Oscar Traynor were wreaking havoc on the 'Tans'.

Tommy Byrne, Quartermaster of 7th Battalion, South Dublin Brigade IRA.

Tom Watkins and Tommy Byrne on active service in Manor Kilbride.

Lewis Sub Machine Gun as used in the Civil War in Blessington in July of 1922.

Blessington Steam Tram line blown up by Republican Troops during the Civil War.

British Troops on the firing range in Kilbride Camp.

The Black & Tans.

Tommy Byrnes premises commandeered by the Black and Tans in 1922.
(Now owned by the Dempsey Family.)

Civil War

THE elected representatives from the 1918 elections formed their own parliament and met in the Mansion House in January of 1919. This was the first Dail. The British response was to arrest the members who were sent to British jails. In the interim period the War of Independence raged and eventually led to the truce. The treaty discussions were complicated by the establishment of the Ulster Volunteer Force in the North who armed themselves with 100,000 guns while the British government turned a blind eye to their activities. The resulting treaty reflected this position accounting for the inclusion of partition in the terms and also requiring the oath of allegiance to the British crown to be accepted.

After protracted discussions the negotiators signed the treaty, which had to be endorsed by the Dail. The imprisoned elected representatives were released and the subsequent debate showed a complete split in Sinn Fein on the issue. With De Valera and Michael Collins leading opposing factions, the treaty was endorsed by a very narrow majority of seven votes. De Valera led his supporters out of the Dail, refusing to take the oath of allegiance to the Crown, as Sinn Fein had spent four years fighting to break the link.

Had the struggle been in vain? He deemed that the acceptance of partition surrendered the fate of Irish Nationalists, in the partitioned area of our Northern Counties, to domination by the Ulster Volunteer Force, who were armed with their 100,000 guns and would be supported by the British military forces. The split led to the seizure of the Four Courts by the De Valera side that became known as the "Republican Troops". The Collins side were referred to as the "National Troops" or the "Free Staters". IRA units split and the civil war had started.

The Blessington unit sided with De Valera. This was a tragic outcome with, in some parts of the country, brother opposed brother. With fierce fighting and bitterness being experienced throughout the land, the National Troops, under pressure from the British government, confronted the Republicans and, with heavy artillery, dislodged them with heavy casualties. Blessington was the rallying point for the re- grouping of the republican force. Their volunteers from Tipperary and Kildare converged on Blessington on July 2nd 1922. The plan was to march on Dublin to relieve the beleaguered force there. National Troops, operating from south Dublin and the Curragh, almost completed an encircling movement around Brittas, Kilbride, and Ballymore Eustace. The Republicans, under the command of Carbury Murphy, had blown up the steam tram line into Blessington and exploded a land mine near Cross Chapel. The National Troops cut off the advance route of the Blessington units by an armed carrier pulled across the road at Crooksling. The entire operation was concluded within a few days with success for the National Troops. Over one hundred prisoners were taken including Andy McDonnell and Gerry Boland, and their arms seized. The others dispersed into the mountains and continued the fight. The prisoners, including members of the Blessington unit, were interned in the Curragh military camp. The Republicans were completely outnumbered by a nationalist force, augmented by recruits who had not participated in the war of independence. There were several casualties among the National Troops, including Col. Dineen who led the force into the town. Some Republicans were killed early in the operation.

With the Republicans in the town were prominent figures such as Gerry Boland, Harry Boland, Sean Lemass and Andy McDonnell, Officers commanding the National Troops, found that the Republicans in Blessington were well prepared with machine guns mounted on the church spire, and a field hospital staffed by doctors and trained nurses who were members of Cuman na mBan was located in an adjoining dairy. They left behind two boxes of hand grenades, several rifles and revolvers. A land mine had been planted on the street, opposite the church, near the Four Stone Tree. The wires led from the church where the Republicans were in occupation. The mine was not detonated. The National Troops intended to bombard the town, but in order to save lives and property, the Republicans withdrew. Seán Lemass, who was later to become Taoiseach, was the operations officer in charge of the Blessington operations. When he left the town with Ernie O'Malley to rally the Republican troops in the South East, he left Tom Watkins in charge of the remaining Blessington force.

Further engagements by the local republican unit consisted of an ambush on National Troops outside the Band Hall in Blessington on Sunday morning, August 20th 1922. About 30 men carried out the attack. Six national soldiers travelling in an armoured car were the targets. Shots rang out when they failed to obey the halt order and the driver, Private Kenny, from Dunlaoghaire, was killed. The officer commanding the troops, Comd. Curley, together with Pt Kelly and two others were wounded. A hand grenade was also used in the encounter. The armoured car and guns were captured by the republican unit.

On September 3rd a land mine was detonated in a culvert under the steam tram line, at Crooksling. On September 13th 1922 the same unit burned Kilbride Camp to the ground. The blaze was seen for many miles around. At the same time they set alight Blessington courthouse with only the four walls left standing. These actions were taken to show that the unit had survived the Blessington showdown in July and that they were still a potent force. Members of the Blessington unit were eventually arrested and interned in the Curragh.

On the national front each side lost many good men. Some were executed and others were assasinated. Michael Collins, leader of the National Troops, was ambushed in Cork and was killed. William T Cosgrave succeeded him as leader of the Provisional Government. The Special Powers Act was introduced and seventy-seven executions were carried out under the guidance of Kevin O'Higgins, who himself was subsequently assassinated,. in a series of retaliatory killings. The Republicans formed an alternative provisional government under the leadership of Eamon DeValera. These desperate events led to the end of the civil war and politics took over.

The Band Hall, scene of the Republican Troops ambush of National Troops on August 20th, 1922, during the civil war.

National Troops sealing off the approach route to Dublin during the confrontation with the Republican Troops in Blessington during the Civil War in July 1922.

Local Transport

LOCAL transport in the village had an intriguing history. In the early days people walked for miles to their destination or the men used horses when they possessed one. The Ascendancy usually had their own horse traps or carriages to convey them from place to place. In addition, hackney car contractors provided a horse drawn car service in Blessington. The mail route from Dublin to Kilkenny and Waterford ran through Blessington. The mail coaches were horse drawn and they changed horses in the town and also collected the mail from Naas for the onward journey. This service was provided by the Bianconi Mail Company.

Horse drawn cars for hire was a business carried on by the Lynch and Garland families at the end of the Nineteenth century. Before that Mr. Kilbee of the Downshire Arms hotel (which is now owned by the Hennessey family) provided the service. Thomas Lynch, born in 1827, moved from the Rathmore area of Kildare to set up his hire Service on the Green. The business was carried on by his son, John Lynch, born in 1866, until the turn of the Century. His stables still exist at the rear of the Byrne family home on the green now owned by Fintan Byrne. The Garland family also operated their car hire business from the village. They originated in Baltyboys and served Col.Smith and Elizabeth Smith in their stately house in the 1840 period. The introduction of the Blessington Steam Tram in1888 was at that time a modern and convenient means of transport. It took its toll of the Lynch and Garland businesses, which closed down in early part of the Twentieth century.

Consideration of the development of a rail service to Blessington was first discussed in 1864 and again in 1880 the plan did not come to fruition until 1888. The initial line ran from Terenure to Blessington and was extended to Poulaphuca in 1895. The introduction of the Tram was welcomed by the local community. It increased trade in the local shops and brought tourists from Dublin to the village and the scenic waterfall at Poulaphuca. It also carried local supplies and transported livestock to Dublin and Dublin Port for export. Some people thought this means of transport was accident-prone. The trackside had many crosses marking the locations of the fatalities. Accidents occurred when pubs along the way closed and inebriated customers fell across the track on their way home. Staff on the tram sometimes fell off as the tram was cornering and many a horse drawn cart was

***Above:* Transport when you come into the world, 1938.**

***Right:* Transport when you are leaving this world.**

upended when the horse was spooked by the sight and sound of the tram. The bodies of unfortunate victims were taken on board the tram and brought to Templeogue Inn, which was beside the tram depot. This pub now bears the name of 'The Morgue' as a result of its association with the tragic side of the Blessington steam tram.

The tram ticket office was a gathering point for the exchange of news and local gossip. Ticket offices along the route were at the Inn at Tallaght, Jobstown Inn, Hamiltons at The Lamb, Blessington and the tearooms at Poulaphuca. The Blessington ticket office was combined with the tram sheds on the green where the Statoil petrol station now stands. The ticket master was Joe Ivors, who lived in the old tollhouse, which is now the Bohan family home on The Green.

In 1929 buses started to ply their trade on the Blessington route, poaching passengers from the steam tram operation. The buses were more comfortable and faster than the trams. Known as the Paragons, the owners of the business were the Paragon Bus Company, they continued until 1931. They were taken over by GOC and subsequently by the Dublin United Transport Company who owned the Steam Tram. In 1934 the famous and memorable '65'-bus route was born, and it still bears this route number into the new Millennium. Extensions to the route were introduced to Valleymount in 1939, Hollywood in 1948, Ballyknockan in 1955, and Donard in 1965. Ballymore Eustace was also Included on the route.

When the steam tram closed down in December of 1932 the tram sheds were acquired by Lar Moore who converted them to a Caltex petrol station and car repair business. These two related events were an indication that the lifespan of the steam tram had run its course. Just as the horse drawn car had been a victim of the steam tram, it in turn had been supplanted by the relentless progress of the motorcar and the bus service. This new development was now the mainstay of transport in the village. Part of the ticket office was now a sweet shop and the other section was used as a dentist's surgery, which older residents will remember, but will never forget. Jimmy Hughes, one of the great characters of the Blessington football scene, subsequently acquired the garage business.

The withdrawal of the steam tram service in 1932 opened up other opportunities. An example was the light freight service which was conducted by the steam tram was now being serviced by the Shirran brothers, Eric and Arthur. They left Blessington each morning for Dublin and returned in the evening in their light lorry with merchandise for the local traders.

"The Morgue" public house in Templeogue where victims of the Blessington Steam tram were brought.

The famed Blessington Steam Tram.

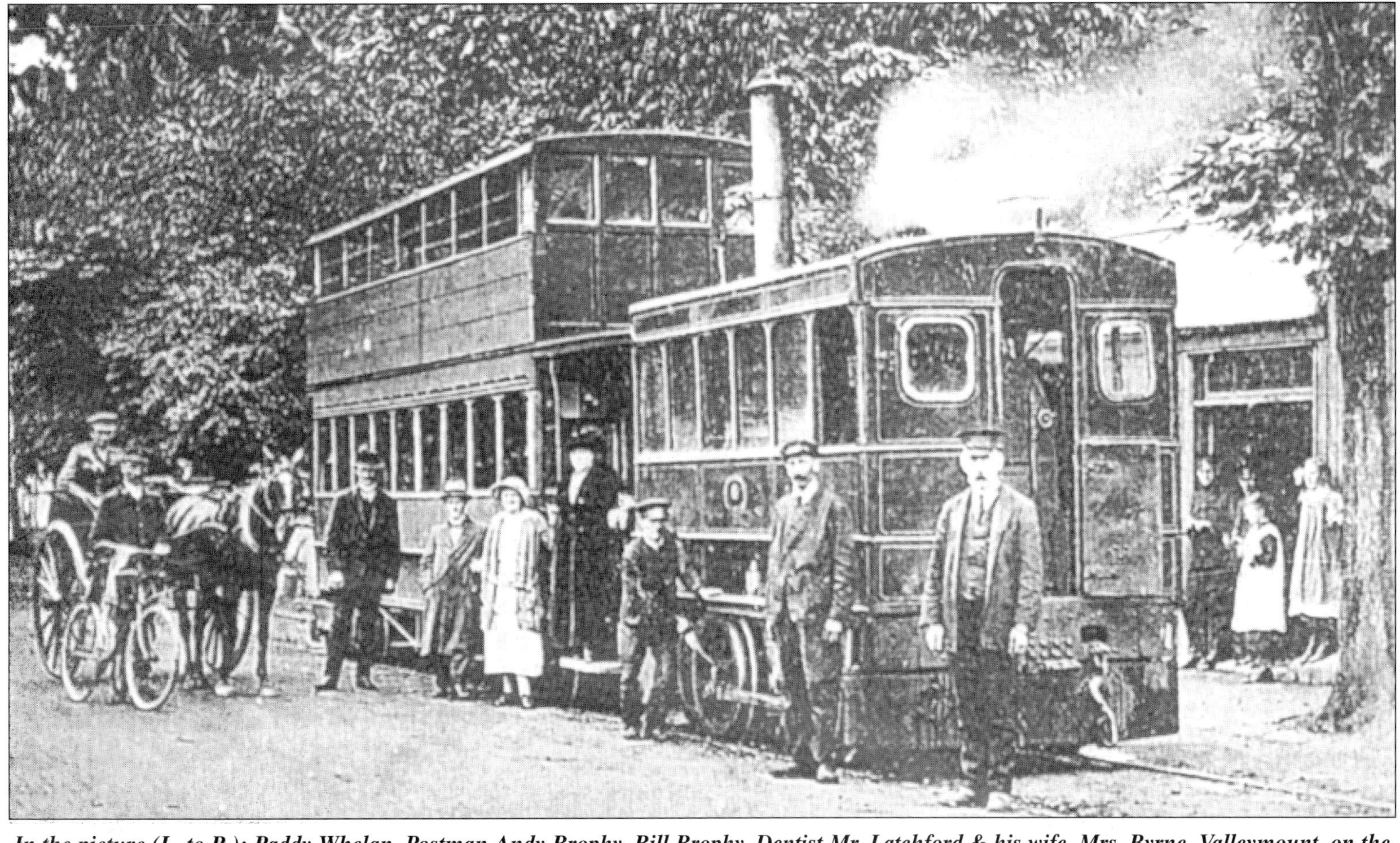

In the picture (L. to R.): Paddy Whelan, Postman Andy Brophy, Bill Brophy, Dentist Mr. Latchford & his wife, Mrs. Byrne, Valleymount, on the step, John Sweeney from Templeogue, Joe Marrie, Joe Ivers, the Ticket Master.
In the door of the office, Bill Nolan, Kit Preston, Molly Moore & Cissie Gelleran.

Left: Johnny Kelly's car.

Centre: The Paragon bus that came on stream in competition with Blessington Steam Tram..

Bottom: CIE Leyland Tiger single decker bus.

Social Scene

IT is probable that early music and dance influence was introduced by the Celts and at a later stage the Anglo Saxon styles. The native Irish versions were derived from these sources but over the years adapted to reflect the culture that developed. The Blessington experience in the nineteenth century was one of two contrasting styles. The tenantry provided entertainment for their own class with music and dance of their own culture, jigs and reels performed to the music of fiddle and melodeon players, while the gentry enjoyed their polkas and waltzes.

The twentieth century started off in similar vein but, with the development of radio and later television, music trends took their lead from American, British and continental sources. Blessington was always up to date with the latest trends. The gentry in Blessington and surrounding areas held sedate musical evenings in their country houses while the tenants amused themselves with dances and music at the cross roads or on stone flags in their farm cottages.

Lord Downshire encouraged a breaking with these traditions of separation in 1847 when he hosted a Big Party for his tenants and to which the gentry were also invited. As the manor house had been burned down in 1798, the party was held in The Downshire Arms Hotel. (Hennessey's). The Kavanagh family, tenants of Lord Downshire who lived in Deerpark, provided the music. Descendants of this family were still playing their music in the nineteen sixties. This social class intermingling was a great success but the social experiment was not maintained.

The Band Hall on The Green was built in 1904 by the committee of the fife and drum band. It was to provide practice facilities for the band and also serve as a Concert and Dance hall for the local populace. Music was simple and innocent and attracted full houses. On occasions music was provided by Jack Moore, Maureen Landers and "Sax" Hanlon, and the locals danced away the night and into the early hours of the morning. Concerts were numerous and very popular.

Concert parties were drawn from the local community. A frequent organiser was William Gyves from Haylands. He had a flair for putting on entertaining shows. Acts that he organised were a "Round the Camp Fire" cowboy group featuring Mick Kavanagh, Paddy Kavanagh, and Eamon Byrne singing Gene Autry songs that were featured in his films. Another act that found favour with the audience was the chorus group of local lads and lassies singing the latest musical songs interspersed with novelty acts. The chorus would sing 'Hey Little

Hen, when will you lay me an egg for my tea' and William would come on stage dressed in a large hen costume, sit on the stage, let out a loud squawk and lay a large egg. His reward was a prolonged round of thunderous applause.

This was the innocent fun, which was the order of the day. Gala Dances to Mick Kavanagh's band were frequent and enjoyable, as was his ancestor's band at the Lord Downshire party many years before. Another frequent visitor to the dance rostrum in the band hall was Michael Keogh's Ballyknockan Accordion band. The big time arrived when Jimmy Dunny played there on his spinnet organ. The band hall was also used for local meetings. Macra na Firma, the Football Club, the ICA, and local branches of political parties held their meetings there. When Blessington Brass Band was formed in 1948, the band hall became its home. The local Boxing club now uses the hall.

As an entertainment venue the band hall was superseded by St Joseph's hall, which was built with Parish funds by Frank O'Toole, a local builder. It opened in 1948 as a dance hall and turned out to be a real ballroom of romance. Very many romances started there, leading to happy marriages and good solid families. The ballroom was opened to the music of Mick Delahunty's band from Tipperary. The big gala dance nights were St. Patrick's Night, St. Stephen's and New Years Eve. Dancing was held also every Sunday night and initially Eddie Quirk's band was in residence for years. Eddie was a bus conductor, lived in Ranelagh and augmented his income with his dance band. His brand of music was very popular and he played there for years. His feature dance tune was "Wait 'Till the sun shines Nelly" and he always concluded the nights dancing with a stirring rendition of "Good night Sweetheart". In the nineteen sixties Elvis Presley and the Beetles were the big influence. With their brand of music came Rock'n Roll and a change of resident band. Capacity crowds came every Sunday night and special buses brought patrons from Dublin. Mick Hennessy' s band from Carlow was now in residency and he lasted for many years.

With the changing style of music came a different style of dancing. Jiving was the order of the day, but only two sessions were allowed per night. Close dancing was prohibited and Fr.Collins and Fr.Lucey enforced the ban by patrolling among the dancers on the dance floor. Failure to comply often resulted in ejection from the hall. Every Sunday night at eleven o'clock the announcement from the stage that the Ballymore bus was ready to leave was the signal that there was only half an hour for the boys to make a move on the girls if they wanted to get a leave home. On the way up to the Dublin bus Johnny Conway's wall was lined with courting couples and resembled the Wailing Wall of Jerusalem.

These were very strict times but a very enjoyable period in peoples lives and this reminder will serve to bring back fond memories. St. Joseph's hall served other patrons besides the younger generation of dancers, variety concerts were frequent and well supported. Artists from the local community performing alongside professionals from the Dublin variety scene and Radio Eireann provided entertainment of a high calibre. A Concert held on the 10th of January featured Mike Nolan, a comedian broadcasting on Radio Eireann, Jackie Cartwright from the famed Theatre Royal and Ann Brennan, a vocalist from the Dublin ballroom circuit all working alongside the Blessington 'Satellite Skiffle Group'. Members of this Local musical venture were, Pete Nolan on drums, Jimmy and Gavin Taylor on guitars, Mick Fleming on tea chest, Fonce Kavanagh on washboard and vocals and Peter Burton on vocals. Compere for the night was an unknown broadcaster who, at the time, was hosting the Birds Jelly sponsored programme on radio. His name was Gay Byrne. His fee for the night was one pound but he was so good he was paid one Pound ten shillings. Exposure at this prestigious venue started him on the road to fame and enabled him to increase his fees and give up the day job.

The opera "Maratana" was also performed there by a Dublin musical society and the hall also was used for a major boxing tournament under the auspices of the Irish Amateur Boxing Association. Din Joe and his famous radio show "Take the Floor" was one of the many high profile events that graced the stage of St Joseph' hall.

In addition to the dance and stage performances, St. Joseph's Hall played host to Blessington's first Horticultural and Craft Show, which was organised by the newly formed Blessington Development Association. On the 18th Of October 1958 the whole community met to demonstrate their talents, and to compete in a spirit of friendly rivalry.

Over100 entries were received for the horticultural competitions, and in a children's painting competition, organised in conjunction with the Leinster Leader, 600 entries were received.

A feature of the show was the display of handwoven tweeds from the newly formed Blessington Handweavers.

All categories in the show were keenly contested and one of the most popular successes was the victory of Mrs. May Tyrell over Sir Alfred Beit in "the best onion competition". This result brought tears of joy to Mrs. Tyrell's supporters. The victory was ironic, as Mrs. Tyrell had been a valued member of Captain Daly's staff in Russborough House in 1932, which was 20 years before the arrival of Sir Alfred to the mansion in 1952.

Members of the Development Association committee were: Rev. Mr. Despard, DD. Chairman, Fr. Lucey, PP. Vice Chairman.

Committee: William Boothman, Myles Balfe, Molly Byrne, Denis Doran, Sean O'Donnell, Toddy Hennessy, Pa. Kelly, Artie O'Leary, Stanley Miller, and James Power.

The population of Blessington attending a party in the Band Hall around 1930.

St Joseph's Hall, the nerve centre of social activity in 1950's and 1960's.

DANCING EVERY
SUNDAY NIGHT
8 to 11.30 p.m.

EDDIE CLIFFORD AND HIS ORCHESTRA

MAPLE FLOOR MINERAL BAR
CAR PARK CYCLE PARK

Admission - - - - 2/6

Buses from Burgh Quay (No. 65) Returning after Dance

(NO DANCE SUNDAY, 6th APRIL, 1952)
(£150 Card Drive Instead).
Tickets 10/-

No 254

YOUR DANCING DIARY 1952

Keep this Diary—it may win you £5 in a Free Draw. See Inside.

DATES WITH IRELAND'S LEADING DANCE ORCHESTRAS
IN
ST. JOSEPH'S HALL, BLESSINGTON

M.C.—SEAMUS DUKE.
Caterer—Mrs. R. BOLGER, Tallaght
DANCING - 9 p.m. to 3 a.m.
Admission 6/- (Supper Extra)

Special Buses from Burgh Quay, Dublin at 8 p.m. each night Returning after Dances.
This Programme is Subject to Alteration without Notice

"Dance Diary" St Joseph's Hall. 1952.

PROGRAMME, 1952

Start the New Year on the right Note with

Friday, 18th Jan. JOHNNY BUTLER & HIS ORCHESTRA with that fine vocalist Frankie Blowers. Personality is the key-note of this Band's outstanding success.

Friday, 22nd Feb. BILLY CARTER AND HIS BAND (from Arcadia Ballroom Bray) One of the really Top-line Dance Orchestras

Sunday, 16th Mar. St. Patrick's Eve PEGGY DELL AND HER BAND (featuring the new Wonder Instrument—The Clavioline). An Orchestra full of life and sparkle with its Leader Internationally famous as a Vocalist and Pianist.

Friday, 16th May STEPHEN GARVEY AND HIS RADIO ORCHESTRA with the Hammond Electric Cinema Organ. A unique combination of Dance Band and Organ under the Master Touch of Stephen Garvey.

Friday, 20th June PEGGY DELL AND HER BAND (featuring the Clavioline) A repeat performance—by popular request.

Friday, 11th July NEIL KEARNS AND THE WELL KNOWN GRESHAM HOTEL (Dublin) ORCHESTRA. A Band with a Big Reputation

Friday, 15th Aug. JOHNNY BUTLER & HIS ORCHESTRA (with Frankie Blowers) You will enjoy dancing again to "Music with a Meaning."

Friday, 19th Sept. SEAN McKENZIE & HIS ORCHESTRA (of Radio Ballroom fame) with Star Vocalist Johnny Keyes (Capitol Theatre, Dublin). If you have heard this Band on the Radio you will certainly want to dance to it.

Friday, 24th Oct. MICK DELAHUNTY AND HIS ORCHESTRA (featuring the golden voice of Mary McCarthy). The personality of its Leader, 10 first-class instrumentalists, and its exceptionally fine vocalist combine to make this Ireland's most popular Dance Orchestra. Admission 8/- (Supper Extra)

Friday, 14th Nov. "Diary Dance"—Free Draw for £5 Note. BILLY CARTER AND HIS BAND Another welcome visit from the Band that has delighted thousands in Arcadia Ballroom Bray. A Cash Prize of £5 will be presented to the patron present at this Dance who produces the copy of the "Dancing Diary, 1952" bearing the winning No. drawn from the drum, together with a paid admission ticket. Members of the Hall Committee or Staff will not be eligible.

Wed., 31st Dec. New Year's Eve. BERT FLYNN AND HIS BAND (Ireland's Leading Song Writer and Composer). With two of Danceland's most pleasing Vocalists—Betty Hurley (winner All-Ireland Vocal Talent Competition, 1950) and Earl Fitzgerald. A First Class Orchestra of Long Established Popularity.

A

DANCE

will be held in

St. Joseph's Hall

BLESSINGTON

SATURDAY, 8TH DECEMBER, '56

★ MUSIC BY ★

Jimmy Dunny's

POPULAR DANCE ORCHESTRA

With Hammond Spinet Organ. Dancing 8.30 to 12.30

Admission : : 4/-

BUS SERVICE AFTER DANCE

Bradley, Printer, Newbridge. Phone 126.

Poster for a Dance in St. Josephs Hall in 1956.

Bucket Factory for the Blessington dairy trade.

Industry

AN area of Blessington situated on the Kilbride road was always known as "The Factory." This was the location of a weaving industry which, unfortunately, ceased operations in 1840. There was also a needle manufacturing operation owned by William Merry which serviced the local weaving factory and similar clothing workshops in Dublin. The other industrial activity in close proximity was flour milling in the Mill House. Other employers in the area at that time were a slate quarry, which supplied slate for Dublin's Georgian houses, a brick factory at Tinode and a copper mine in Kilbride. Flanagan's, Darker's and Doran's sandpits provided good employment. They were subsequently taken over by Roadstone. The sand and gravel from these pits built Dublin City.

In 1957 weaving was revived in Blessington. Fr.Daniel Lucey, the parish priest, set the project rolling when he acquired a traditional hand loom and installed it in the Band Hall where hand weaving classes were conducted by Mr. McNelis, a Donegal traditional weaver.

Funding for the project was secured from Archbishop Charles McQuaid and was administered by a committee, which included Tommy Byrne, Dinny Doran, Sean O'Donnell and Sean Newman from Kilbride. Financial support was sought from Wicklow Co. Technical Education Committee who were not in a position to help. Marketing advice and support was given by Mr. Jim Hackett of the Botany Weaving Mill, Dublin, Mr. Kane of Kane & Co. Handweavers and technical advice was given by Mr. Reddington of Gaelteacht Industries.

The first trainee was Vincent Byrne, who moved on to an administrative position in The Botany Weaving Mill, and the first cloth produced was a wine colour velour with a white fleck.

When sufficient trainees were fully trained the operation moved to a converted barn in Doran's yard. Construction work was carried out by local volunteers just as they had done in the development of the local football pitch for the football club. The industry had found a permanent home.

Commercial production began in July of 1958 and the product range included dress tweeds, heavy outerwear tweeds, quality scarves, rug tweeds and furnishing materials. Blessington Handweavers were in full production.

It was not all plain sailing for this fledgling industry. The Blessington venture did not receive any state aid and survived on its profits and local endeavour. The Government did however introduce heavy subsidies for the textile industry, but only in The Gaelteacht areas. Blessington was being depopulated at the time by persistent emigration but did not qualify under this scheme for financial assistance. It did suffer badly from the effects of the introduction of this scheme as the subsidized competition was now in a position to undercut prices on the home market.

Blessington Handweavers carried on for many years but eventually succumbed to the winds of free trade in the 1960's when even the well-established leaders in the textile industry could not compete with cheap imports from low cost countries. An exercise in self help, in depressed times, did not get its just reward.

Classic Clothing Company set up a garment manufacturing operation at a later stage but it also wilted, as the force of competition from Asian low cost producers captured the Irish market.

With greater appreciation of the requirements of small communities, the Industrial Development Authority assisted in the development of small industrial estates and Blessington was to benefit from this. Food processing, stone finishing, ink manufacturing and paint manufacturing flourished in the area as a result of state intervention. Alas this assistance came too late for Blessington Handweavers, but perhaps this experiment in self help highlighted the need for concerted action by state agencies to stimulate the growth of small local employment ventures.

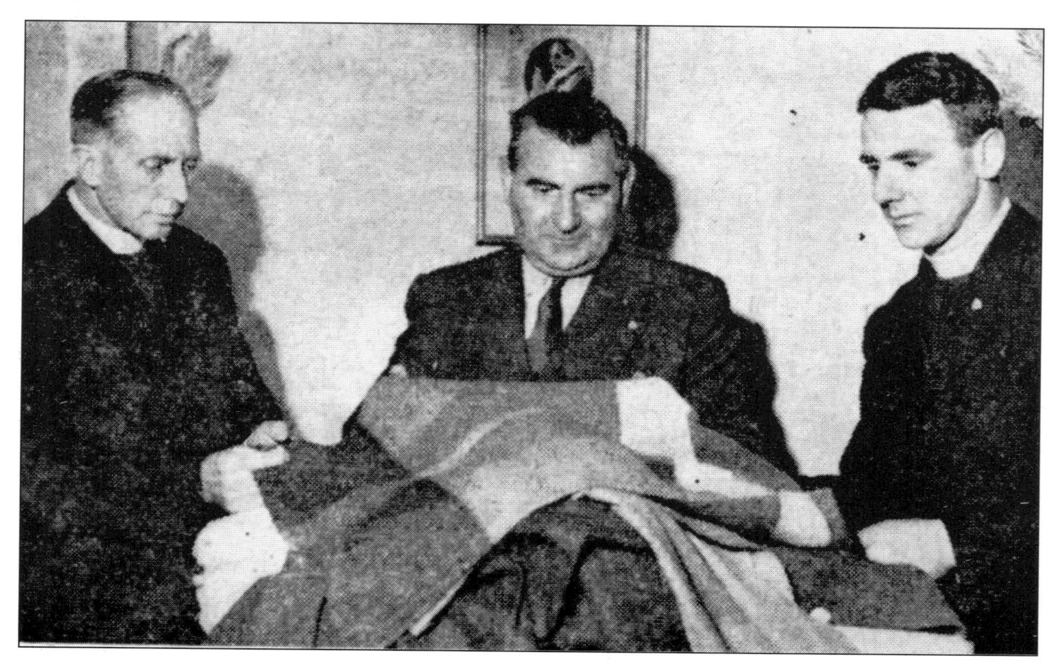

Some of the cloth made by the Blessington Weavers being examined by Very Rev. D. Lucey, P.P., Blessington, Mr. Denis Doran, and Rev. J. Collins, C.C., Manor Kilbride.

She Taught Them All

ONE of the most influential people in Blessington's history retired in October of 1960. Mrs. Lilly O'Donnell was teacher of 'baby infants' and "high infants" in the National School for 45 years. A native of Shanagolden in Co. Limerick, she took up her duties in 1915 in the old National School. The principal of the school at the time was Mr. Landers. She taught her pupils on their introduction to the real world in their most formative years and did so with great sensitivity and care

Front row: *Mag Carroll and Maisey Nolan.*
Second row: *May Hamilton, (nee Clarke). Bernard Hanlon, Mrs O'Donnell, John Carroll, (Glashina) Molly Finnegan, (nee Flanagan).*
Third row: *Mick Tyrrell, Odey Flannagan, Molly Byrne, (nee Moore), Charlie Doran, Bridie Fleming, (nee Nugent), Odey Tyrrell, Kitty Nolan.*
Fourth row: *Jack Tyrrell, Jim Hamilton, Dinny Doran.*

Mrs. O'Donnell was a legend in Blessington and her preparation of pupils in spiritual matters equipped them with a good foundation on which to build worthwhile lives, based on strong Christian principles. In 1936 the new school was built and Mrs. O'Donnell transferred to it to continue her mission in life. On her retirement in 1960 about 400 well-wishers and ex pupils gathered in St. Joseph's hall to show their gratitude and appreciation of the influence which she had on their lives.

The group photograph is of her first and last pupils, a graphic indication of her lifetime's work.

The presentation committee was Fr. Crinion, PP. Fr. Collins CC. Mr. Jim Quinn. School Principal, Mrs. Molly Byrne, Dinny Doran, Jimmy Hughes and Jim Hamilton. Former Parish priest, Fr. Lillis and former curate Fr. Supple returned to pay their tributes on this historic occasion.

Her husband, Sean O'Donnell was manager of the local Employment Exchange and was a noted Irish language enthusiast and teacher. They lived on the green with their three sons, Colm, Michael and Manus. Mrs. O'Donnell received messages of goodwill and best wishes from ex pupils who over the years had dispersed throughout the world.

Confirmation class of 1942.

Girls Confirmation, 1948.
Front row: Sadie Brophy, Eilish Geoghan, Teresa Egan, Mary McGrath, Tess May, Anne Doyle, Margaret Duffy, Maureen Byrne, Una Byrne, Bridie Coughlan, Betty Byme.
Back row: Bridget Gilheany, Teresa McNamara, Annie Geoghan, Pamela Burke, Colette Behan, Cosy Daly, Shelia Shannon, Eileen Jones, Peggy Merrins

First Communion Class of 1945
Front Row: Buddy Young, Jim Murphy, Joe Egan, Pete Nolan.
(Back Row): Paddy McGee, Eilish Geoghan, Brendan Byrne, Vincent Byrne, Sheila Broe, Paddy Daly, Odey Tyrell.

Blessington Fyffe and Drum Band, established in 1904. This ensemble was the predecessor of the Brass Band.

Blessington Brass Band

BLESSINGTON brass band was established in 1948. The organizers were, Tommy Byrne, Frank O'Toole, Jim Clarke (senior), Lar Moore (senior), and Jimmy Miley. These were the same people who were, at various stages, in Blessington Gaelic Football club in the village.

Secondhand instruments were procured in Rathdrum, Co. Wicklow by Tommy Byrne, who worked in the council offices at the time. He discovered them in an old press in the AOH Hall in the town. The organizers raised the required funds and purchased them. They were in bad condition but usable. They were sent to Williams Bros. in Eustace St.in Dublin for restoration.

The committee set about assembling the membership of the band. The initial membership was composed of a mixture of a few people with some brass band experience, but the majority of the new recruits never played a note of music in their lives. It was from this motley crew that evolved a significant and successful brass band that achieved many notable appearances in its lifetime. Jim Smith was appointed conductor and tutor of the band. A native of Waterford, but by now living in Walkinstown in Dublin, he was an accomplished trombone player in the Garda Band. His musical qualifications were awarded to him by the London College of Music. The material he had to work with was a few ex musicians from the old Ballyknockan Band, i.e. Jim Flynn, Tom Mc'Evoy, Jim Mc'Evoy and Larry Byrne. The rest were hopefuls with plenty of enthusiasm but devoid of any musical knowledge.

Practice nights were on Tuesdays in the band hall on The Green, which had been built at the turn of the century by the old Fyffe and Drum band, which performed with distinction in the area. No doubt, the ghosts of music past were in the background encouraging and supporting the new venture, which would maintain the musical tradition of the village.

Initial public appearances of the band were Church parades, Corpus Christi processions and local football matches. Recitals at concerts in St. Joseph's Hall and also at the famous Four Stone Tree in the centre of the village. They also led the parades at Leinster championship matches and inter county games throughout the county. Other notable appearances were the leading of the Anti Partition Parade down O'Connell St. in Dublin in 1955 and at the Republican Plot at Arbour Hill. The salutes were rendered by Jim Flynn. The band also led the parade at the Parnell celebrations at Avondale, and also performed at civic

Brendan, Eamon, Vincent and Fintan (front), members of the Byrne family who played with St. Josephs Band.

week celebrations in Glasthule in Dublin, and competed at the national brass band championships.

When Jim Smith retired and returned to Waterford, he was replaced by Ned Cannon, also a member of the Garda Band and, subsequently, by Mick Clarke, who was one of the initial raw recruits to the band. The wheel had turned a full circle. Another of these recruits, Brendan Byrne, graduated to become a cornet player in the Garda Band, and toured America with them. He was following in the footsteps of his old mentors Jim Smith and Ned Cannon.

Throughout the lifetime of the band, it was sustained by various fund raising events. The band committee was assisted in its endeavours by a ladies committee. Prominent in this support group were Bridle Tyrell, Jane Flynn, Molly Byrne and May Breen. Sports events, dances, concerts, flag days and jumble sales were features of these activities. One amazing incident occurred at a jumble sale. Sean O'Toole and Vincent Byrne went out on their bicycles collecting jumble for the event. On calling to Ballyward House to canvass support, they were met by William McCauley, the owner, who asked them to wait and he would see what he could do to support their efforts. A few minutes later he returned with a young racehorse, handed it over and stated that this was his contribution. The two boys brought the horse along the road behind their bicycles to the Band Hall. Willy Doran stabled the horse until the day of the jumble sale where it was auctioned. It resulted in a major contribution to band funds.

Another unplanned, and unexpected, source of funds was a contribution from the public at a summer recital at **The Four Stone Tree**. On a sweltering hot Sunday afternoon, at the end of a rendition of the tune "Pennies from Heaven", Jim Flynn took off his band cap to cool off and left it on the ground. Suddenly, there was a constant trickle of coins from the public, who interpreted his gesture as a collection, and proceeded to fill the hat. The band members put their own interpretation on the occurrence, claiming that it was for a round of drinks, in appreciation for the performance.

A notable feature of the band was the number of family members that participated. They were, Eamon, Brendan, Vincent and Fintan Byrne, Jimmy and Mattie Ryan, together with their father, Mattie Ryan (senior), Pat and John Brennan, Tom and Jim McEvoy, Mick and Paddy Kavanagh, Mick Clarke and his son Tony, Jim Breen and his son Seamus, Jim Flynn and his sons Con and Jimmy. Other Members were Larry Byrne, Sean Tutty, Denis Bohan, Pa Tyrell, John Aylward, Billy Crowley, Sean O'Toole and Jimmy Craul.

The economic depression of the seventies resulted in the dispersal of the core membership and the band ceased to exist in the nineteen eighties. Its demise ended a notable contribution to the fabric Blessington culture.

Inaugural assembly of St. Joseph's Brass Band.

Blessington Brass Band.

Back Row: Paddy Kavanagh, Larry Byrne, Seán Tutty, Dennis Bohan, Jim Breen, Pa Tyrell, Eamonn Byrne.
Middle Row: Mick Kavanagh, Matty Ryan Snr., Tom McEvoy, Pat Brennan, Jim Flynn, Jimmy Ryan, John Aylward, Billy Crowley, Matty Ryan Jnr.,
Seated: Mick Clarke, Brian Clarke, James Clarke Snr., Fr. Union P.P., Conductor – Jim Smith, Frank O'Toole Snr., Jimmy Miley, William Gyves.
Front Row: John Brennan, Brendan Byrne, Seán O'Toole, Vincent Byrne.

The Band at Parnell Celebrations in the 1950s.

Blessington Brass Band leading the Anti-Partition parade down O'Connell St. Dublin in 1955.

Blessing of band instruments.

Blessington Lakes

TALES FROM THE DEEP

THE riverbed and valley, which were the residue of the glaciers, were to prove a major amenity and service opportunity for Ireland and Blessington thousands of years later. It did, however, require human intervention to alter the appearance and function of the river to achieve its perceived potential.

After the War of Independence and the treaty with Britain the native Irish Government took over the reins of power in 1922. At this time there were proposals on the Cabinet table for two competing electricity generating schemes. One was the Liffey proposal for Blessington and the other was to harness the river Shannon. The Shannon Development won the day as first priority and was built at Ardnacrusha in 1925 The Blessington proposal had its merits. The requirement of a generating source close to the major electricity consumer, Dublin city, coupled with the requirement of Dublin Corporation for a major water supply for the city ensured that the Liffey development would not be far behind

The enabling legislation to give the go ahead for the Liffey project was passed in 1936. It was steered through the Dail by the minister responsible, Sean Lemass, who was on duty in Blessington in July of 1922 as part of the Republican Force that was holding the town. Building started in the autumn of 1937. The construction contract for the dam to be built at Poulaphuca was awarded to a UK company, François Cementation Co.Ltd., from Doncaster. They supplied the expertise and project management. Local labour was employed and approximately 200 wage earners were working on the site.

While the creation of the lakes was a major alteration to the local landscape, it was the disruption of the inhabitants and their subsequent re-location that caused major upheaval and a major moral dilemma for the ESB. Not alone were the local residents disrupted from their homes but their dead relatives were disturbed from their graves. A burial rights committee was formed to negotiate with the ESB and to represent the views of relatives of the deceased who were buried in Burgage Mor Cemetery, which was to be submerged in the flooding operation. The graveyard was below the high flood line. Land ownership that was manifest during the ascendancy period was stoutly defended, but on this occasion the beneficiaries were to be their own fellow countrymen. Eventually deals were done, the families moved, and progress continued unabated.

A very positive side of the project was the fact that workers on the construction sites brought their families to live in Blessington, and made a very positive contribution to the economic development and the social fabric of the community. Local people found gainful employment in times of little opportunity. They acquired new skills that were to carry them to worthwhile achievements in their personal lives. Overall the creation of the lakes and the hydroelectric facility was achieving its objective as a development for the greater good.

The infrastructure of the locality was altered for all time, with the destruction of old roads and the quaint bridges that spanned the river. These were replaced with new roads and modern bridges.

The blowing up of the old bridge at the Mill Bank in Blessington brought back nostalgic memories to the local people. Many a romance started at this picturesque meeting point beside the old Mill House. It was landmarks such as this that provided the location for the exchange of local gossip, news and opportunities for social interchange Scenic beauty did not start with the creation of the new lakes. The Mill Bank was a place of outstanding character.

Located in the valley between Knockieran and the wooded slopes on the outskirts of Blessington Village, it provided the perfect location for the old corn mill. The mill was built in the days of the Downshire Reign in the village. It provided a valuable service to the local tenants, who farmed the fertile land along the river banks of the Liffey. It was operated by various millers throughout its lifespan Recorded occupants in the early days were, Thomas Ebbs in 1850, William Smith in 1874, William Ebbs in 1884, George Barker in 1895 and Edward Moore in 1902.

Edward Moore lived there with his wife Mary (nee Clarke) in the Mill House. They had two children, Molly and John. Mary Moore died a young woman when the children were very young, John died in his youth and Molly was sent to her aunt, who was married to John Lynch, the hackney car driver, on The Green. When Molly reached adulthood she married Tommy Byrne who played a part locally in the war of independence. Edward Moore got married again to his sister in law, Kate Clarke, and they had one daughter, Nora who in turn married Walter Shirran. At one stage the Dowling family also lived there.

The mill was a four-storey structure with adjoining living accommodation. Part of the milling machinery was housed in the basement section. It was driven by a millwheel, which was 14 ft. in diameter. The water buckets were 2 ft. wide, with the overall width of the wheel was 5 Ft. The energy to drive the wheel was provided by the water flow along the millrace falling on the mill wheel from a drop of 5 ft. The shaft rose through the 3 floors driving the millstones and the screw. The corn entered the mill at road level, progressed through the process and exited at the top floor in sacks, lowered on a winch to the waiting horse and cart for transportation back to the farm

The mill was sacrificed to the demands of progress, was submerged and now stands beneath the water surface. When there is a fine summer the water level drops and the chimney of the mill emerges from the deep as an eerie reminder of times past

Blessington Bridge before the flooding

The Creation of Blessington lakes. After the flooding.

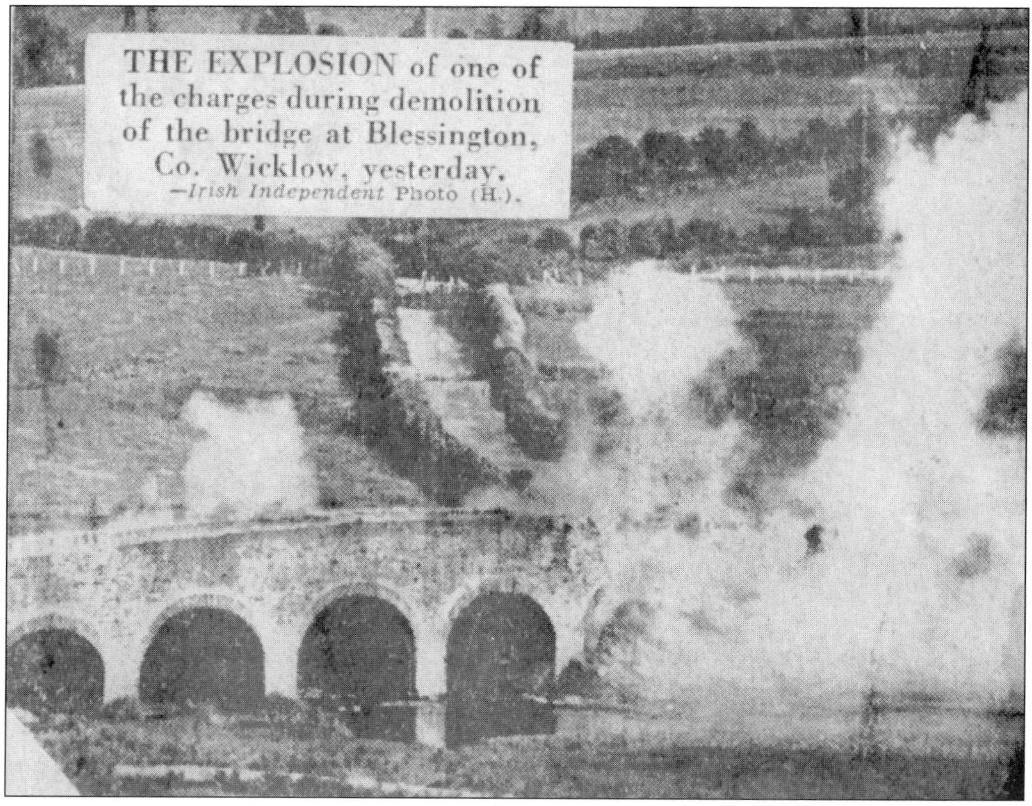
THE EXPLOSION of one of the charges during demolition of the bridge at Blessington, Co. Wicklow, yesterday.
—Irish Independent Photo (H.).

"The Big Bang"
The demolition of Blessington Bridge by the army.

"The Mill House", submerged under Blessington Lake during the creation of the Hydro Electric Scheme in 1939.

Blessington Bridge and Mill House prior to flooding.

Lar Moore: Founder Member of Blessington Football Club in 1910, was a playing member up to 1914. He was chairman of the club, and was also chairman of the West Wicklow Board for many years. He was a Labour member of Wicklow County Council. A Founder of Blessington Brass Band and was its Chairman up to the time of his death on January 24th 1951.

Blessington GAA

UP THE BLUES

UP the Blues was the war cry of the loyal band of Blessington football supporters throughout the years. Fathers, mothers, sisters, brothers, sons, daughters, uncle Pats and aunt Nellies always turned out to urge their heroes to victory for the honour of their small village. A lot of fervour and emotion was invested in this local institution. As Blessington grew in size to its present status of a large expanding town, the growth in support and passion intensified, commensurate with the vast increase in population. This was a just recognition of the sound foundation which was laid by the creators of the club many years ago, and for their successors up to the present day, who spared no effort or commitment to keep the momentum going.

The club has an interesting and colourful history. This is an account of its inception, the culture from which it evolved and the history and geography from which this local movement sprung. It gives a flavour of the social backdrop of Blessington in 'these rare old times and a snapshot picture of the great characters who were involved over the years. It is a look at its successes and failures, its achievements, its missed opportunities and, in particular, its survival

The Gaelic Athletic Association was founded in Thurles, Co. Tipperary, on the November 1st 1884 by Michael Cusack and Maurice Davin, supported by 13 other enthusiasts.

Football was of course played extensively all over the country prior to this date. The Thurles meeting was to put a formal structure to these activities and also to include athletics, which was flourishing at the time. It took some time for this initiative to come to fruition and it took about 2 years of gradual momentum for the association to bed down and become a formidable force, and grow to the heights that it has attained.

Like any other new organization it had its growing pains, dissentions and difficulties but withstood the tests. In the first two years, two of the original founders had resigned as a result of disputes between two factions who were seeking dominance. They were the Irish Republican Brotherhood on one side and the National League, who were controlled by the home rule party on the other side. By 1887 it had over 600 clubs registered through 11 county boards, spreading its wings in the following years.

Blessington 1916 County Senior Champions.
M. McDonald, J. Clarke (Goal), J. Cullen, L. Behan, W. Cullen, E. Fitzsimons, J. Murphy, P. Loughlan, A. Hannlon, T. Ryan, P. Cullen (Capt.), A. Behan, G. Murphy, P. Whelan, D. Conway.

Wicklow affiliated to the association in 1885 with a registration of 36 clubs. At the inaugural meeting held in the Town Hall, Wicklow on St.Stephen's day 1886 Blessington was not represented at the meeting. It is not clear how many of these clubs were active or how many were paper clubs, created to establish voting strength at conventions on behalf of the opposing factions. A nationwide slump in club registrations was reflected in the fact that by 1889 only one club was attached to the Wicklow county board. The election of Luke O'Toole from Bray to the position of general secretary of GAA in 1901 sparked a revival of interest in the association and in affiliations in Wicklow.

Political developments, however, were a diversion in the 1914 period with the establishment of the Irish Volunteer Movement. Young men were faced with the dilemma of a division of their time and commitment resulting in another gradual slump in GAA activities. This persisted up to 1922 but Wicklow and Blessington managed to keep going and complete their programmes.

The Blues came on the scene in 1910. The organisers of the club were: Martin McDonald, Maurice Landers, Lar Moore, Paddy Behan, Andy Hanlon, Tommy Lynch, Bill Mooney, Peter Cullen, Bill Brophy, Tom Clarke, Gerry O'Sullivan, Donal Monaghan, Paddy Hanlon, Charlie Cullen and Paddy Whelan. With a victory over Kilcoole in the junior championship of 1914, it was an indication that they were plying their trade either individually or collectives in the neighbouring counties of Dublin, and particularly, in Co. Kildare prior to their registration with the Wicklow Co. Board. The skills demonstrated by players such as Larry Behan, Paddy Cullen and Andy Hanlon, who gained their place on the Wicklow team that same year, were not just acquired in the four years since 1910.

Blessington moved up to senior level the following year and proved to be a major force. In west Wicklow they defeated Hollywood, Valleymount and Baltinglass and qualified to meet Wicklow Town in the final. The period of 1915 was an unsettling time, and for various reasons the final of 1915 was not played until 1916. On Sunday July 30th 1916 Wicklow Town and Blessington met in the senior County final. This was just 14 weeks after the 1916 Rebellion. The match was played in Laragh and started 45 Minutes late. The team that lined out that day was a strong accomplished combination that was fit and well prepared for the fray. The team was Peter Cullen (captain), Jim Clarke in goals, Jim Walsh, Tom Ryan, Jim Cullen, Martin Mc Donald, Ned Fitzsimons, Kit Whelan, Andy Hanlon, Willy Cullen, Larry Behan, L. Hanlon, Paddy Whelan, and Dinny Conway.

The Blessington team dominated the game from the start and outclassed their opponents in every department. Larry Behan opened the scoring for Blessington with a well-taken point. This was followed by a point by Andy

Wicklow Senior Football Team – 2002.
Blessington players – Back Row: Fergus Daly (third from left), Barry O'Donovan (end of row) – Front Row Jonathan Behan (first on left).

Hanlon. Blessington reached the interval with this 2 points lead. On the resumption Paddy Whelan slotted in a fine goal after 5 minutes. Shortly after, Larry Behan increased the lead with a well-taken point. Wicklow then forced the pace and had a narrow miss when the ball rebounded off the crossbar. Continuing pressure by Wicklow was rewarded with a point scored by Tom Cullen. This was to be Wicklow Town's only score of the game. Larry Behan added another point and Blessington ran out deserving winners by a score of 1 goal and 4 points to 1 point for Wicklow Town. Blessington had won their first Wicklow senior football title.

They were back again in 1917. The team that dominated this period was, Jim Clarke, Jim Cullen, Andy Hanlon, Larry Behan, Martin McDonald, Willy Cullen, E. Fitzsimons, Tom Ryan, Paddy Cullen, Andy Behan, G. Murphy, D Conway and team captain Paddy Whelan. Tinahealy beat Blessington in the final of the senior football championship of 1917. Peter Miley Gerry O'Sullivan Jack Tyrrell and Joe Tyrrell played on that team, while Andy Hanlon, Declan Walsh and Gerry O'Sullivan were operating at county level during the same period.

GAA fixtures were very much curtailed all over the country during 1920 to 1923 due to the War of Independence and civil war activities.

Inter county honours for individual Blessington players continued throughout the 1920's but team honours evaded the club until 1928. A new crop of skillful players had emerged in the interim period. Ned Harte, Joe Delaney, Bill Redmond, Artie O'Leary, Johnny Byrne, Johnny Brophy, Jim Conran, Hugh Hamilton, Jimmy Dowling, Odey Tyrrell, Tom Hamilton, and Tom Clarke came on the scene, and, under the captaincy of Martin McDonald, they captured the 1928 Intermediate football championship, in great style, beating Newtownmountkennedy. Jim Hamilton played in the goals, and Tom Hamilton was man of the match. The score was Blessington 3-4 to Newtown's 1-3. The 1928 final was delayed and was in fact played in Roundwood in April of 1929.

1931 brought on another great batch of players who were to emerge as some of the notable characters of Blessington football. Ginger Brophy Mick Kavanagh, Barney Flanagan, Charlie Doran, Jack Murray and Jim Plant made their first championship winning appearances while joining Tom Clarke, Artie O'Leary, Hugh Hamilton, Odey Tyrrell, Tom Hamilton and Jim Hamilton to win the 1931 junior Championship. Odey Tyrrell was man of the match on this occasion. The team returned to senior ranks in 1932 without success but Tom Hamilton was hitting the headlines with sterling displays for the Wicklow county team. A good run in the 1933 senior football championship, reaching the final, but giving Roundwood a walk over, conceding the championship. There was a long delay in setting a date for this encounter. By then they were unable to field a team due to injuries and loss of players to other clubs.

Fergus Daly

Jonathan Behan

Barry O'Donovan

Fragmentation of clubs was a development of this era with new teams springing up for short periods and then disappearing. Ballinatona, Liffey Rovers and Cross Chapel made brief appearances during this time.

Notable new players to join the squad to win the 1936 intermediate championship were, Charlie Doran, Jimmy Dennison, Mick O'Neill, Christy Clarke, Bill Fleming and Frank O'Toole, who had returned from America, having married Mick O'Neill's sister, Peg, in New York. Frank, a native of Rathdangan, had inter county experience with Kildare. He was on the panel of the great Kildare team that won the 1928 and the 1929 All Ireland senior finals. He came on as a sub in the 1929 final and got a full team place in the senior ranks in subsequent matches in the same league season.

Moving up to senior level, they were defeated by Rathnew in the 1942 final. A few new faces made their appearance at this level. They were Liam Halligan, Paddy Kavanagh (Mick Kavanagh's brother), and Toddy Hennessey Prior to his debut as a senior player Toddy had proved himself in under age competition and had gained his place on the county team in 1939 and 1940.

By 1946 Blessington were back to intermediate level where they were once again successful in the county final decider. The line out (including subs} was: Toddy Hennessey, Mick Kavanagh Jimmy Hughes, Tom Shannon, Mick Clarke, Jack Keogh, Jimmy Stones, Paddy Kavanagh, Bill Fleming, Jim Kavanagh, Pat Quinn, Jack Murray, Jackie Bohan, Christy Clark, Jimmy Denison and Odey Tyrrell. A feature of this team was the inclusion of three Kavanagh brothers and the first appearance in a final for Jackie Bohan, Pat Quinn and Jimmy Hughes. The following year, 1947, Jimmy Stones and Toddy Hennessy had claimed their rightful place on the county junior team while Halley O'Donnell made it to the county minors.

Next honours to be claimed by the Blues were again at intermediate level and the year was 1949. This team included, for the first time, players from Manor Kilbride who had, by this time, amalgamated with their fellow parishioners in Blessington. Mick Quinn from Ahfarrell, Stephen McGrath and Joe Eustace augmented their Blessington colleagues, who also added Paddy Halligan, Liam Halligan's brother, and Jack Pointz, a stylish footballer from Monaghan who had come to Blessington to join the staff of the local bank. They beat Kilcoole on this occasion. Toddy Hennessy and Jack Pointz featured on the Wicklow team that captured the Leinster junior title in 1949, beating Meath by one point (5-2 to 2-10) in Croke Park. In the same year another O'Toole, Frank junior, appeared on the scene by making a major contribution to the Wicklow minor team.

Up to this stage Blessington was operating very successfully at intermediate level, with occasional forays into the senior and junior ranks. Tom Carroll

Jimmy Hughes.

played with the county junior team in 1950 while Tom O'Hagan and Frank O'Toole (junior) performed well for the county minors.

1956 was to be the year of the minors. The first sign of things to come was in 1955 when Blessington beat Baltinglass in the final of the West Wicklow championship, only to be deprived of honours on an objection which was upheld by the West Wicklow board. Baltinglass went on to win the county final that year. The Blues made no mistake the following year and beat their old adversaries, Baltinglass, in the first round by a margin of 2 goals. They went on to beat Dunlavin in the regional final, Tinakilly rovers in the county semi final to qualify to meet Ashford in the county final. Blessington had not reached a minor final since 1936 when they were beaten by Bray Emmets in a closely contested game.

This 1956 final was played in Aughrim as a curtain raiser for the senior final and resulted in a victory for Blessington by a score of 3-8 to 3-4. The game was a thrilling encounter, which overshadowed the senior final. The team that did their duty on that day were Pat Fleming, Tommy Kavanagh, Paddy Magee Jim Murphy, Brendan Mahon, John Brennan, Aidan Gilheany, Mick Fleming, Jimmy Kelly, Gabriel Murphy, Gerry Cullen, John Murphy, Peter Clarke, Peter Daly, Vincent Byrne. John Brennan was captain. Subs were Sean Duffy, Bernard Lillis and Brendan Byrne. Scorers for Blessington were Jimmy Kelly (1-4), Peter Clarke (1-1), Mick Fleming (1-01, Vincent Byrne (0-2), Peter Daly (0-1). Referee was the legendary Eamon Fitz Moules from Annacurra. Peter Clarke went on to play for Wicklow at senior level and railway cup honours for his province.

Toddy Hennessy.

There was an exodus from Blessington on that day by car and a fleet of special busses. Ashford had to contend with a very vocal group of Blessington supporters chanting the traditional war cry "Come On The Blues" this support was invaluable late in the game when Ashford made a late rally but the boys in blue, conscious of what was expected of them, held out to win by the winning margin of 4 points.

Throughout the 1956 campaign the Blues were a prolific scoring team, with a total of 13 goals 23 points for, 6 goals 11 points against. Prominent supporters at the game were, Mick Kavanagh, Frank Moore, Sledger Hughes and Dinny Doran, whose son John went on to be an inter county referee and travelled to Australia to referee the International Compromise Rules games. Also to the fore were Paddy Daly, Bill Fleming, who made an influential contribution on the playing field in the 1940's. Chairman of the club, Fintan Gilheany was also prominent and ably represented the entire club membership in this hour of glory. It was also inspiring to have Jim Clarke senior, one of the founders of the club and goal keeper on the 1916 senior championship winning team, on the mentors bench willing the team to victory. Who could resist the pleading of Jimmy Hughes, a great stalwart of the club, for this one victory. The man who made it all happen, Toddy Hennessey, shed a quite tear of pride and, without exception, the team dedicated great victory to their manager, Toddy, without whose skill, guile and belief, this victory would not have been achieved.

The club President, Fr. Lucey had anticipated the result and produced from the back of his car a crate of champagne, which was consumed with great abandon. John Brennan and Mick Fleming gained honours at county level that same year.

In October 1957 Frank O'Toole junior starred for the Wicklow county team, when they won the O'Byrne cup final, before his home supporters at Blessington. This was a special game for Frank and a proud occasion for his father, Frank senior, who had divided loyalties on that day. Wicklow won that final by a score of 2-9 to 1-10 for Kildare, a team that Frank senior played for 28 years earlier. Frank junior also donned the blue and gold in the first round of the Leinster championship against Dublin in Athy that same year.

The 1970s were barren years but the next generation were learning their trade and were beginning to assert themselves. Blessington as a town was expanding, the national economy improving, new families were taking up residence which strengthened club membership and ensured that the support base was there to enhance the administrative element of the clubs activities.

Some fine footballers who had not got the opportunity to play on championship winning teams were the backbone of the club's survival. Players such as Billy Brennan, Pat Brennan, Sean O'Toole, Francis O'Toole, Jack Boothman,

Liffey Rovers – 1934.

The Team was based in Manor Kilbride and was a combination of Kilbride and Blessington players, which resulted from Blessington's inability to field a team for the Final of the 1933 Wicklow Senior Football Championship.

Front row: Martin Murphy, Mick Byrne, Peter Kelly.

Middle Row: Odey Tyrell,, Jack Cooper, Eric Sherrin, Scan Newman, Alister Mitchie, Ned Carroll, Joe Lynch, John Brennan.

Back row: Jack Collins, Barney Flanagan, Christy Dennison, Tom Flanagan, Myley McGrath, Patrick Benson, Daniel Dunne, Thomas Plant, Joseph Benson.

Blessington Intermediate team 1938. Photo of team and supporters taken in Hollywood.

Front row: Jack Tyrell, Christy Hanlon, Jim Kavanagh, Paddy Halligan, Christy Clarke, Bernard Hanlon.

Middle row: Christy Dennison, Matty Ryan, L Cummins, Jack Tyrell (Forge) Liam Halligan.

Back row: Tom Hamilton, Christy Maguire, Ned Harte, Bill Fleming, Jimmy Graham, Miley Balfe, Pa Tyrell, Paddy Hughes, Jim Hamilton, Mick Neill, Toddy Hennessy.

Mac Boothman, Tom Byrne, Frank Moore and the Reynolds brothers, Mick, Peter and Johnny all played great games for Blessington. Francis 0'Toole was constantly claiming his place on the County team and Jack Boothman was to make his mark on the national stage at a later stage.

The tenacity of the players and administrators began to pay dividends, and lady luck smiled once again, when Blessington captured the Wicklow junior championship crown in 1974 by beating Carnew in Aughrim. Many of the players were the sons or grandsons of former Blessington stalwarts. A new generation had arrived on the scene.

The Team doing duty on this occasion was: S. Sargent, M. Hennessy, J. Hennessy, M. Doran, P. Donoghue, T. McGrath, P. Quinn, J. McGee, A. Hennessy, T. Cullen, J. Finnegan, P. Finnegan, P. Murphy, S. Breen and D. Byrne. Subs on duty were A. Doran, P. Sargent, D Kennedy and C. Nolan.

This feat was repeated against the same opposition 5 years later at the same venue when they captured the Intermediate football crown. The victorious team was: J. Finnegan, F. Byrne, P. Donoghue, N Hennessy, S Sargent, A. Doran, T. Cullen, P. Quinn, R. O'Donnell, T. Murphy, P. Sargent, R. Hennessy, P. Keenan and J. Magee. The team was managed by Frank Flanagan.

1979 was a vintage year for the club and they also captured the junior championship fielding the following team: B. Finnegan, A Halligan, and J. Toomey. J. Coogan, N. Sargent, N. Shannon, P. Hanson, D. Hennessy, G. Walsh, S. Ahern, A. Hennessy, N. Sargent. F. Flanagan, C. Shannon, S. Ellis and S. Breen.

The minor team also reached the County final but lost out to Baltinglass, and was also Under 21 finalists, being defeated by the same opposition. The senior team continued their winning ways, reaching the 1980 final but again experienced defeat by Baltinglass. They suffered the same fate in 1981 being beaten by Dunlavin in the senior football decider. They had fielded teams to reach county finals in five grades that same year but came away without any silverware. This was a magnificent performance by one club and despite the fact that they did not savour any of the final victories; they had earned the admiration and respect of all the clubs in the county.

1983 was a year of determination and focus by the mentors. It was 67 years since Blessington were crowned Wicklow senior football champions. Despite near misses in 1932 and 1933 the major title proved to be an elusive prize. The appointment of Tommy Carew, the Kildare mid fielder, as coach was an inspired move. He had played 130 games for Kildare and scored a total of 38 goals and 138 points in the process. He represented Leinster in the Railway Cup campaign in 1972. They got down to strategic planning to make 1983 the year of destiny. After a tough assignment against Hollywood they marched to Aughrim to confront the "old enemy", Baltinglass on September 25th.

Blessington Minor Football Team – Wicklow Champions 1956.
Front row: Fr. Lucey, Tommy Kavanagh, Peter Clarke, Vincent Byrne, Gabriel Murphy, John Brennan (Captain), Jimmy Kelly, Gerry Cullen, Jimmy Hughes.
Back row: Mick Kavanagh, Paddy McGee, Aidan Gilheany, Mick Fleming, John Murphy, Brendan Mahon, Peter Daly, Jim Murphy, Pat Fleming, Scan Duffy, Bernard Lillis, Brendan Byrne.

Veterans of victorious Blessington minor football team who captured the County Championship in 1956, at the Anniversary Dinner in 1996.
Surviving members: Pete Murphy, Mrs. Nina Fleming, representing her late husband Pat, Mick Fleming, Peter Daly, Peter Clarke, Fintan Giheany who was Chairman of the club in 1956, John Brennan, captain of the winning team, Brendan Mahon, Paddy McGee, Phyllis Murphy, representing her late husband John Murphy, Eilish Murphy, representing her late husband Jim Murphy, Vincent Byrne.

It was a close fought encounter. The line out on that memorable day was: Dermot Hennessy, Ciaran Shannon, Paddy Sargent, Paddy Quinn, Shay Sargrent, Paddy Lennon, Pat Quinn, Ronan Hennessy, Martin Shannon, Robert Boothman, Kevin Hanlon, Pat O'Toole, Patsy O'Donoghue, Tom O'Hagan and John Finnegan. Tommy 0'Hagan was man of the match as a result of his goal that brought Blessington across the line to gain victory by a score of 1-10 to 1-6.

The experience of Pat O'Toole and Pat Quinn, supported by the young bloods of the team, carried the day and eventually outplayed Baltinglass in every sector of the field. The Half time score of 1-4 to 0-3 in favor of Baltinglass did not auger well for the blues. They did however spark into their true form in the second half and the mid field supremacy of Pat O'Toole and Dermot Hennessy, feeding a rejuvenated forward line, that made the difference in the end.

After two lapses in the first half, which resulted in two flattering scores for Baltinglass, the Blessington backs regained their composure and shut out the opposing forward line to great effect. Pat Quinn was an effective target man at full forward and his distribution skills were used to great effect when winning high balls and laying off to his colleagues in scoring positions. Scorers for Blessington on the day were: Tom O'Hagan, 1-1, Pat O'Toole, 0-6. Ronan Hennessy, 0-1, Dermot Hennessy, 0-1, and R. O'Donnell (who replaced Paddy Sargent), 0-1.

The backroom boys had done their job well. Team trainer, Frank Flanagan and coach, Tommy Carew, had instilled in the team the importance of fitness and stamina and this proved to be the difference between the two teams in the end.

Frank Byrne, Jack Boothman, Pete Nolan, Paddy McGee, Jimmy Hughes and their colleagues on the committee joined with all their longtime loyal supporters on the victorious exit from Aughrim with the team to join the faithful at home who extended to them a heroes welcome. The surviving players of former years were at the forefront of the victory celebrations. These were the people who had kept the blue and white flag flying in the lean years and it was fitting that, in many cases, it was their sons who had delivered the ultimate prize on this September day.

A massive reception awaited the Heroes and a cavalcade of cars escorted the victorious team into the town to a tumultuous reception by an ecstatic local population. .It was a long road from 1916 to 1983. It was 27 years since the club had captured their first minor title. The spirit of the mentors, supporters and the players who gave so much of their energy and the sacrifices made by their wives and families was surely vindicated in September 1983. That day is now firmly established in Blessington folklore.

Blessington Senior Football Team – winners of the Wicklow Senior Football Championship 1983

Front row: Martin Shannon, Bob Boothman, Kevin Hanlon, Pat O'Toole Patsy O'Donoghue, Tom O'Hagan, John Finnegan.

Back Row: Dermot Hennessy, Ciaran Shannon, Paddy Sargent, Shay Sargent, Paddy Lennon, Patrick Quinn Ronan Hennessy, Pat Quinn.

Blessington Junior Football Team, winners of the Wicklow League Championship 1969/70.

While that championship victory was the pinnacle of the club's achievements, Blessington went on to establish hurling by winning the 1983 junior hurling championship to cap off a memorable year. Victory in 1985 followed but the 1990's went by without success. The new millennium brought victories in the junior football Championships of 2000 and the junior championship of 2002.

The administration of the club was always in the hands of a hard core of dedicated men and women who espoused the nationalistic ideals of the Gaelic Athletic Association and had a deep love of sport. Despite adversity, they financed and nurtured the club and provided a focus for the exuberance of the young men who flocked to team activities at a time of little wealth or job opportunities.

The 1940's and 1950's were tragic times for clubs throughout the land, with the constant haemorrhage of young men in their athletic prime departing for jobs in The UK. and America. Blessington club did not escape this unfortunate de-population trend but nevertheless managed to weather the storm and survive. Just as the players had demonstrated on the field of play, it was the tenacity of the administrators that brought the club through this period intact.

THE FIELD

It was during this decade that the present football pitch was acquired and developed. The club had been renting a field from Biddy Hyland at the Jots, near Burgage, just off the Blessington-Baltinglass road. Practice was on an ad hock basis each evening in Doran's paddock beside the old church. It was completely un-organized, with players of all grades and abilities mucking in together. Some good talent emerged from the mayhem that existed. In 1945 Bill Boothman, a very strong supporter of the club in particular and the GAA in general, provided land beside the new cemetery in Burgage at a cost of £800. His sons, Mac and Jack, played for the club and were lifelong members. Bill Boothman travelled all over the country in support of the teams and the sport he loved. It was not surprising that he came to the aid of his club in their quest for a permanent home of their own. This was not the last contribution that this family made to the GAA.

Development of the ground was now a priority. The first phase was the fencing, which brought comfortable accommodation for the spectators. The players were now the priority. In those days the only facility for players to "tog out" was in the nearest ditch or behind a convenient bush. This situation was not exclusive to Blessington but was the norm through the country. As a player,

Toddy Hennessy was only too well aware of the discomforts endured by the young men in pursuit of their passion and, now that he had moved into club administration, he was determined to do something about it.

Toddy spearheaded the dressing room project and inspired the club members to give their services on a voluntary basis. Members of the club congregated at the pitch, after work in the evenings, to develop the site with picks, shovels, wheelbarrows and plenty of sweat. It is this spirit of self-sufficiency, which the GAA evokes, that inspires the membership to overcome the little difficulty of fund shortage by investing their time and energy in order to achieve their objective. This is the quality that makes the organization different from other sporting Organizations.

The block laying was done by 'Sledger' Hughes, the roofing and carpentry by 'Pa' Tyrrell, and plastering by Francis Hughes. They were aided by the goalkeeper, backs, mid-field and forwards doubling as labourers to get the .job finished. The facility that resulted from these endeavours was a far cry from the hedges and ditches that were in general use at the time, and brought the pitch to a standard that was attractive to the Wicklow county board and the Leinster council.

In addition to national league matches scheduled by the Leinster council, Blessington football club sponsored their own 4 county football competitions and the Father Lucey Cup inter club tournament as a means of raising funds to defray the expenses incurred in the acquisition of the grounds. The club realized that gate receipts on their own would never clear the debt. They organized a series of concerts, dances, and card drives which augmented cash flow from football sources. The magnitude of the financial commitment, when development and running costs were added, made the committee decide that the raising of funds was to be a priority. Eventually the debt was cleared. In later years the dressing rooms were extended and the pitch levelled, resulting in a football grounds that was fitting for a great club.

"THE PEOPLE"

The continuity of the administration personnel of the club is an indication of the deep roots that were implanted by the founders and their supporters. Longevity of service was a feature of the input of Blessington mentors and the handing on of the baton to their sons and daughters ensured that the future of the club was secure. Families such as the Clarkes, Tyrrells, Kavanaghs and Hennessys have been represented for many years.

Jim Clarke senior was a founder member of the club. He played on the

1914 successful intermediate team and was goalkeeper on the victorious Blessington senior team of 1916. He was on the committee all down the years and was vice president up to his death on 29th Dec. 1963, aged 82, a span of service over six decades. His sons Tom and Christy played in the 1935 and 1945 teams. Another son Jim played for Wicklow in 1940. His grandson, Tony Bird played for Blessington and Wicklow at minor level in 1964 and at junior level in 1965.

Odey Tyrrell represented Blessington on the Wicklow Junior team in 1933. He played on the Blessington team that won the Wicklow intermediate championship in 1928 and the junior championship in 1931. He played on the senior team that contested the 1942 county final when they were defeated by Rathnew. Playing continuously on the Blessington team, he again appeared on the intermediate team that won the championship in 1946. Odey then moved on to club administration and was an active member into the 1960's. His service to the club spanned over thirty years. At the age of 72 years he passed away on May 26th 1978.

In 1921 John Metcalfe, auctioneer, sold the premises known as the Downshire Arms to Arthur Hennessy from Naas. The new residents made a lasting contribution to Gaelic Football in Blessington. Their son Toddy was to make a significant impact on and off the field. He made his appearance at minor grade for Blessington in 1938 and for Wicklow in 1939, and again in 1940. He was on the Blessington team that contested the 1942 senior football final and on every team at junior, intermediate and senior levels that the club fielded up to 1949, when he was called to duty for the Wicklow junior team that won the Leinster title that year.

Toddys next big day was as manager and coach of the Blessington minor team that won the Wicklow title for the first tine in the club's history. The players dedicated the victory to Toddy as a just reward, not just for his contribution to the team on that day but to his contribution to the very survival of the club over the years. Along the way he married Elsie Moore from Grangecon. Elsie, a member of a great Gaelic family who were also well known in greyhound circles, was to go on to make a notable contribution to the club in her own right. After his playing days Toddy continued to inspire the club membership up to his untimely death on the 23rd Feb. 1987.

The whole Hennessy family was involved in the GAA. Toddy's sister, Beth married Liam Halligan, who was playing for the club in the early 1940's. Three of his sons. Arthur, Martin and Jerry played on the victorious team that captured the Wicklow junior championship in 1974. Martin was joined by two other sons, Ronan and Dermot, on the intermediate team that was crowned champions in 1979.

Ronan and Dermot represented the Hennessy family on the Blessington senior team that made history in 1983. Mrs. Elsie Hennessy was the matriarch of the club. She carried on the inspirational role where Toddy left off and was held in very high esteem by all members of the club, young and old, and received the admiration and respect of all football folk throughout the county. She was the recipient of a special award at the ceremony to present the county championship medals to the minor team of 1995, and the presentation of mementos to the previous minor champions after a gap of 40 years. The younger generation of Hennessys are presently involved in the club at player and administrative level and Elsie Hennessy has left the club in safe hands.

The Kavanagh family contributed 4 brothers to the Blessington football scene as players and administrators. Mick Kavanagh first played for the club in 1930 and was a member of the 1931 junior championship winning team. He played for the senior team in 1932 and 1933. He performed continuously in all grades up to the late 1940's. He was joined by his brother Paddy on the teams in 1942. Jim Kavanagh joined the fray in 1946 and by Fonce Kavanagh in 1954. Mick Kavanagh was a staunch club member and after his playing days were over he was a very effective and influential chairman of the club. At a time of very little transport in the 1950's Mick was always available to transport players in his mayflower car.

Mick was a plasterer by trade. While earning his living at his trade and pursuing his career as a talented footballer, Mick also kept up the family tradition of running his own dance band. Both Mick and his brother Paddy were founder members of St. Joseph's Brass Band. He was a very versatile and talented man. He will be remembered with great respect throughout the county.

Another character of Blessington football was Jimmy Hughes. A legend in the club and much further afield, his contribution to the success of the club was enormous. His vigour and enthusiasm was infectious and he had the younger members of the club struggling to keep up. On the playing field Jimmy was a journeyman player, putting in solid consistent performances. He first entered the records as a player in 1946 on the intermediate team that captured the county championship. After a prolonged playing career, Jimmy was to make his mark as a county board representative of the club. He caused consternation among the other delegates in his insistence on a better deal for his club and for West Wicklow football. On the County board he formed an alliance with "Hack" Byrne of Baltinglass to fight for a fair deal for the west. Up to this point, the board was dominated by East Wicklow clubs.

Jimmy was a 'hands on' administrator who tended to take the short route to achieve objectives. He certainly got things done but unfortunately, at times, things did not go according to plan. He will always be remembered as the dedicated club man for whom his sport was his life. Jimmy died in 1999.

Paddy Magee was from Kilmalum and was a member of the 1956 minor team. He was a mighty full back and subsequently played at intermediate and senior level. He joined the club committee in 1957 and is still a prominent member in this new millennium.

Fintan Gihheany was chairman of the club in 1956 and was still an active member of the committee 40 years later. He presided at the presentation ceremony to the survivors of the 1956 victorious minor team at a function In the Downshire House Hotel in 1996.

Pete Nolan has also the same length of service and he is also a current member of the committee that has brought the club to its present strong position.

Augmented by livewire Michael Sargent, who made a major contribution as treasurer of the county board, Frank Byrne. Gerry McIntyre and under the watchful eye of Jack Boothman the club has a very bright future. With development plans well advanced for another re-location, this time to the Demesne, the club has the potential to be the model that other clubs will follow.

The younger generation have carried on the proud traditions of their predecessors on the playing field. In the 1980's Pat Quinn emulated the achievements of his father by being the dominant force at midfield for Wicklow. The 1990's saw the rise of another crop of football stylists to make an impact on the inter county scene and do their club proud. Jonathan Behan, Barry O'Donovan and Fergus Daly wore the blue and gold with great distinction, as did Martin Shannon, and set the standard for future generations to follow. Pat O'Toole, who played for Dunlavin and Blessington, represented his county and Leinster in the railway cup competition. At under age level club members were also making their contribution. Bob Boothman, Peter Daly and Tom O'Hagan at under 21 and Gary Richardson, at minor grade, also made appearances for their county.

The vocational school also made its contribution to the Gaelic Athletic Association ethos, and won many county championships. It served as a nursery for aspiring talent. Under the watchful eye of Gerry McIntyre and Willie Hendricks underage players were well catered for and ensured that "The Blues" were well capable of retaining their pivotal role in Wicklow football.

From a shaky start in 1910, through the struggles of the 1940's, to 1970's and the emergence of the GAA as a dynamic national institution in later years, Blessington Football club played its part in the development of the National game.

Blessington GAA Grounds, 2003, at Burgage.

Mr. President

IN the year of 1963 Blessington football club registered a young player who had returned to his native village having successfully completed his education and sampled the joy of his first employment opportunity as a Vet. This young man was Jack Boothman, son of Bill and Jane Boothman who farmed at Troopers Fields.

The Boothman family name goes back many hundreds of years as residents of the town and was involved in all aspects of the developments since the creation of Blessington. They are truly natives and it was not surprising that Jack was to leave his mark on local history.

Jack Boothman, Blessington GAA club member President of GAA 1994-1997.

He was born in 1937, was educated at Kings Hospital in Dublin and graduated from the veterinary college in 1959. While he was starring on the rugby fields he could not be registered as Gaelic footballer. This, however, did not stop him from occasionally turning out for Blessington minors and juniors. Both Jack and the club were content to leave this little detail to Jimmy Hughes who somehow overcame the problem in his usual fashion.

Jack became an official "GAA man" in 1963 when he succeeded Pat Quinn as secretary of the club. He cut his administration teeth in this position and it is said that he developed his legendary sense of humour during this period. He soon graduated to the position of chairman. His commitment and work rate came to the notice of neighbouring clubs, resulting in his elevation to the Chairmanship of the West Wicklow board. He was following in the footsteps of Lar Moore, one of the founders of Blessington football club, who served in this position for many years previously.

His progress did not stop at district level. Having served as a delegate to the county board, and being a hands-on member, he progressed to the position or Vice Chairman of the county organization and was subsequently a representative to the Leinster council. During this ascent he was still chairman of his local club and had a major input into the club's winning of the 1983 county senior Championship. He inspired the young players in their quest for inter county honours, which they did with great success. He served as vice-chairman of the provincial body for many years and became its chairman from 1987 until 1989.

While it was usual for administrators of the GAA to be perceived as being divorced from the grass roots, Jack Boothman's performance was being noted by ordinary club members throughout the country and was recognized as an official that was tuned in to their concerns. Greater demands were being made on players and it required a "player's man." at the top to address the problems.

In his quest to bring a new focus to the GAA, he contested the presidency at the end of John Dowling's reign in office in 1991 but was narrowly defeated by Peter Quinn of Fermanagh. The vote on this occasion was close. Geographical factors had entered the equation as delegates were not keen to have the presidency go to a Leinster county for two successive terms.

Jack, while disappointed and unfortunate, was to have his day in the sun. At the 1993 congress he was elected to the presidency of the Gaelic Athletic Association and commenced his term of office in 1994. It took him thirty one years to progress from the hot seat of Blessington football to the hot seat of the national organization, a just reward for the perseverance and hard work of a true Gael who proved to be a worthy successor to Michael Cusack.

The Boothman presidency was different and timely. His focus was on the players and youth, which had been overshadowed by the development demands of Croke Park and other provincial venues. He recognized that you had to develop players to play at top level in the newly developed grounds. His support for the clubs was legendary and he travelled the length and breath or Ireland to encourage and support the herculean efforts of club members, their wives and girlfriends who gave so unselfishly of their time and energy in the cause of the national sport which they loved.

Youth and school football was similarly supported to ensure that there was an ongoing supply of talent. His policy of appointing coaches was inspirational and will his legacy that will ensure the successful survival of the sport. His recognition of the threat of competition for the allegiance of the youth from other codes was timely and resulted in policies that made membership of The GAA a badge of distinction.

In the popularity stakes Jack had a close competitor in the person of his wife Nuala. Her contribution to his success was enormous. He benefited from her encouragement and unstinting support in the task he successfully accomplished by the time of the completion of his term of office. The organization owes her a debt of gratitude.

Jack Boothman is still the guiding light of Blessington football. He attained the second highest position in the land. Perhaps it is time that he considered seeking the highest position for which his background and performance at national level makes him eminently suitable. How about it Jack?

Jack Boothman. Blessington GAA club member President of GAA 1994—1997.

"On parade" President Boothman introduces President Robinson to the teams at the All Ireland Hurling final, 1996 – Wexford v limerick.

Local Defence Force

IN 1939 Hitler invaded Poland, Britain invaded Europe and the LSF invaded O'Leary's field. World War Two had started. While the rest of the world had a war on their hands, Ireland had a bit of an emergency. Comforted by our status as a neutral country Ireland as a nation did not participate in the conflict. Many thousands of Ireland's young men joined the British army and fought with British regiments.

Local security was a concern. The Irish Army was by this stage well established, as was the Garda Siochana. An Sluagh, an auxiliary group, was established in 1934. The Government decided to create a type of home guard in 1939, which they called the LSF, to support the Garda Siochana. This arrangement was not ideal and responsibility for this body was transferred to the army, who changed the name to the Local Defence Force (LDF).

Blessington had its own company of the LDF who performed their duties with great efficiency. Members of this force were not paid but fulfilled their task out of a sense of national duty. Local businessmen, tradesmen, farmers and public servants answered the call and established a cohesive unit. The purpose of this force was to act as a surveillance group and to impede any adversary in the event of invasion.

When Neville Chamberlain declared Britain's entry to the conflict it became obvious that they were vulnerable to attack by the Germans from the west and that the Germans would have scant regard for Ireland's neutral status. British and American forces had the approaches from the Atlantic covered but there was a fear that German infiltrators could land in Ireland from the air and make their way to Britain as saboteurs. That was where the LDF proved their worth.

The Blessington unit made an assessment of the situation and identified fields on which German planes could land. O'Leary's field was first on the list. The LDF planted tar barrels at regular intervals throughout the field, providing a serious hazard for prospective invaders. Other identified landing spots got the same treatment. They mounted a permanent watch on the lakes, as intrusion by water landing aircraft was possible. Plane spotting and identification was part of their duties and information gleaned from these activities proved useful to the allied forces. Many German and British aircraft got lost and strayed over Irish territory. One such aircraft crashed on the Wicklow Mountains and the four occupants were killed. The Blessington LDF were involved in the recovery operation.

On 14th Of April 1941 a British Hampden Bomber, returning from a bombing mission over Berlin, lost their bearings over Yorkshire, got lost and continued on over the Irish Sea. The Garda in Blessington heard the lost aircraft over the town at 4.00 am and the crash occurred shortly after on Blackamore Hill, near the rebel camp of 1798.

The airmen were identified as Kenneth Hill, John Lamb, Frederick Erdwin and Steven Wright. It was ascertained that the victims were of the Protestant Faith and were given a Christian burial in the Church of Ireland cemetery in Blessington. Their Union Jack draped coffins were carried in funeral procession into the church by of the Irish Army, who afforded full military honours.

The Blessington company was commanded by Bill Boothman. Other members included James McKiernan, the local chemist, Frank O'Toole, the local builder, Sean O'Donnell manager of the local labour exchange, Jim Quinn, principal of the national school, Paddy Whelan, a prominent footballer and many other young men from the area. They wore very smart uniforms and drilled on a regular basis.

Sean O'Donnell and Jim Quinn, members of the LDF in their uniforms.

On occasions they performed ceremonial duties. At the opening of the Church of Our Lady Of the Most Holy Sacrament in the village in 1943, they provided a guard of honour for Archbishop McQuaid, who performed the Consecration. Subsequently they frequently paraded through the village and were a common sight headed by their one man band, Mick Kavanagh playing rousing marching music on his Piano Accordion. How times have changed.

After the war the

Government awarded emergency service medals to the volunteers, the ribbon was red with a white central stripe.

The Blessington Company of the LDF performed a very important function during the war. its close proximity to Dublin made a very important cog in the circle of surveillance around the capital. The sweep of the searchlights over the city, perfectly visible in Blessington, was the signal that alien aircraft were in the area and was a call for the LDF men to man their stations and be prepared for any eventuality.

The contribution of the LDF, as a national body of about 100,000 men throughout Ireland, served the country well. Although neutral, their activity was an indication to the free world that the nation was vigilant. The information gleaned from their observations was regularly passed to the allied forces and was invaluable in the mapping and tracking of enemy flight patterns.

The LDF was disbanded in 1946 and was replaced by the FCA as a dedicated army reserve. Blessington made their contribution to this new force under the command of Jack Kearney and Charlie Geoghan.

1959 Glen of Imaal – 6th Batt FCA. (Artillery). Aidan Cruise, John Coogan, Andy Doran, Mick Doran, Billy Hamilton, Con Flynn, Charlie O'Connor, Pat Fleming, Charlie Geoghan, Tommy Richardson and many other Blessington men are included.

"RAF Funeral" 1941. Cortage proceeding down Main Street of Blessington.

Union Jack draped coffins entering St.Mary's Church escorted by the Irish Army.

Farming

MIXED farming was predominant in Blessington up to Ireland's accession to the Common Market in 1973. After that specialisation was necessary to devote all available resources to intensive production methods, thereby increasing yield and revenue. Farming at last began to thrive. It was not always like that.

Two acts of the British Parliament, which related to the land question in Ireland, had a profound effect on land ownership. The first of these pieces of legislation was the Land Act of 1881. Up to this stage a tenant who was giving up his tenancy due to old age or illness had to surrender title back to the Landlord. Now they could sell the tenancy and realize an asset that they built up over the years of hard work and good management. The second Act was the Wyndham's Act of 1903. This piece of legislation permitted tenants to borrow 100% of the price of the land from the state. As times were getting tough for the absentee landlords, they were glad to exit with guaranteed payments. These Acts were passed as a result of campaigns, which were pursued with great vigour by Daniel O'Connell and Henry Grattan.

Farmers in Blessington availed of the new arrangement and for the first time had security of title. Repayment of these loans was made by annual land annuities to the British Government. Payments continued up to the formation of the Irish Government in 1923, but with great difficulty as was to be expected in a fledgling state.

Fianna Fail came to power in 1932, DeValera withheld the land annuities, Britain retaliated by imposing penal duties on imports from Ireland and so started the Economic War. As Ireland had not got a strong industrial base, it was the small farmers who took the hit.

Farmers in Blessington were involved in dairy farming, dry stock and to a lesser extent tillage. The hill farmers were rearing best quality Wicklow sheep,while householders in the village reared a pig, hens, chickens for their own consumption and turkeys for the Christmas market.

Rabbit trapping was also a source of income. Paddy Flanagan of the Red Lane dispatched a twice-weekly supply of rabbits to Hanlon's butchers in Moore Street in Dublin. Blessington was also a reliable source of supply for pigs to the Dublin market. Turkeys reared by the housewives in the village found a ready market at Christmastime. The men folk would call around to the houses where they would hold their card schools, with the turkeys as prizes. These were great Christmas social events.

There were no supermarkets or door-to-door milk deliveries in those days. Local farmers ran their own dairy parlours where locals went each evening for their requirements. Gyves Eagers Dorans and Q'Learys supplied the residents. Milk was not pasteurized but was water-cooled and all milking was done by hand. The bulk milk was collected daily by Hughes Bros for supply to the Dublin market.

The small milk buckets used by local residents were supplied by visiting Tinker families who visited Blessington on a regular basis. Prominent highly skilled Tinkers who visited the area were Luke Wall, his wife Ally and his extended family. These people were highly respected and were always given a gracious welcome. The Wall family burial plot is in Burgage cemetery and is marked by an imposing marble edifice.

Farming at harvest time tended to rely on community involvement and reflected the rural nature of interdependence and neighbourly assistance, which was part of Irish culture at that time. With the benefit of hindsight, one can look back at the romantic landscapes of the cornfields and hay fields full of industrious farm families and their neighbours sowing and reaping the crops that would take them through the year.

Willy Dorans farm was typical of the mixed farming that was pursued in Blessington. They had a herd of Friesian cows, and dry stock. They grew potatoes and turnip root crops and on the cereal side they grew crops of oats, wheat, and barley. The essential crop of hay also featured in their crop production. This mixed harvest ensured that they were self sufficient in feed and fodder for their livestock during the winter months.

The farm machinery of the 1930's & 1940's was a far cry from the sophisticated equipment of today. The example of Dorans farm would be indicative of all the rest. In the spring they used horse drawn ploughs and flat bed harrows to prepare the ground for crop sowing. Potatoe and turnip fields were drilled and farmyard manure spread. The turnips and seed potatoes were set by hand. After germination the turnips had to be thinned out by hand. This was a backbreaking exercise, as was the potato picking.

Hay making in the summer was an enjoyable period in the farm calendar. In August all hands would be pressed into service to save the hay. Neddie, Dorans white draft horse would pull the mowing machine to cut the hay and do a similar task with the tumbler to turn the hay, and the buck rake for gathering the hay, which was then built into 'cocks' prior to transportation by bogey, drawn by Neddy, to the hayshed.

Highlight of the haymaking day was the arrival of Mrs. Doran on her bicycle, cycling down the field with two baskets of home made brown bread and home cured bacon sandwiches. These were washed down with bottles of fresh buttermilk. The menu consisted of all home produce as deli-counters and supermarkets had not yet been invented. At meal break the workmen were entertained by the birdsong of the Lark, the Curlew and the croak of the Corncrake. Mrs. Doran would then depart to prepare the evening meal for the workmen, on their return after an arduous days work in the hayfield.

The harvesting of the grain crops was carried out in similar fashion with one exception. When the crops of wheat and oats were brought to the farmyard the grain had to be separated from the straw. This gave rise to the biggest event in the farmer's year, 'The Threshing'

The threshing was a communal effort. Martin Murphy would arrive in Dorans yard with his powerful steam engine and threshing machine to perform the task in hand. On completion, he would carry on to Eagers farm and then on to the Gyves farm. For all three thrashings the farmers pooled their resources of manpower and there was a great buzz of excitement and activity. These were also great social occasions with an exchange of views and opinions on the problems of farming, on sport, politics and world events.

The commercialization and specialisation in farming, together with the advancement in farm machinery design, has denied to us these great occasions, which have been consigned to folklore and history.

The farmers were caught in a bind. The land annuities were, in a way, the monetary price of independence. Because of the underdeveloped state of the industry, the State had not got the resources to continue the payments and claimed that, in any case, they were unjust and immoral. The retaliatory action of the British meant that Ireland had no market for agricultural products.

Evidence of the economic war could be seen on the street of Blessington. Fair Day was held on the main street of Blessington on the 13th of each month when farmers brought their cattle, sheep and pigs to sell. Their customers were other farmers who were re-stocking, or cattle dealers who bought the livestock for export. Local butchers, John Cruise, Miley Cullen and Pat Quinn were also significant buyers at the fairs.

When the trade war started, the number of cattle sold diminished dramatically and the farmers had to bring their livestock home unsold. It had become a buyers market which was exploited to the full by the cattle dealers. Cattle smuggling became the order of the day. The dealers bought stock at derisory prices, smuggled them across the border and sold on to the British market at unpenalized prices. Vast fortunes *were* made at this time by the dealers at the expense of the farmers.

Fair Days in Blessington were great social occasions. Public houses owned by "Love' Mullally, 'Gunch" Byrne, Biddy Dowling, James Power, Jimmy Miley, and Arthur Hennessy did a roaring trade on these days. It was an opportunity for an exchange of views, gossip and a bit of craic. Roving minstrels and street traders always put in an appearance, which added to carnival nature of the day. Nellie Moody and her sister, who lived at the Red Lane, ran a tearooms in a premises beside the Garda station for the convenience of the farmers.

Breaches of the law on Fair Days usually consisted of drunkenness, the odd row, "found on licensed premises after hours", and the serious crime of having no light on a bicycle. These type of breaches of the law were handled in a sensitive manner by Sgt. James Bohan and his gardai John Brennan, Martin Murphy and John Armstrong, who served in the station during this period

On the trade front 'tit for tat' duties were being imposed by both Britain and Ireland until common sense prevailed on both sides. Talks ensued, a deal was struck on the question of the Land Annuities, sanctions were lifted and the economic war ended in 1938,.with mutual benefit to the protagonists.

Trade slowly recovered and farm development started to evolve. National farm organizations such as Macra Na Firma and young farmers clubs were organized in Blessington and provided a forum for discussions on the direction that this sector had to take.

The first tangible evidence of change was the demise of the Fair Day and the introduction of the cattle mart. Blessington was at the forefront of this development with the opening of one of Ireland's first marts in "Mullaly's field", in November of 1955, by the Doyle brothers from Donard. The first cattle drover for the sales ring was Mikey Ryan from the Green. This location could not cope with the rapid expansion of the venture and soon moved to Murphy's field at Holy Valley on the outskirts of the village.

Irelands free trade agreement with Britain in 1965, and accession to the European Common Market in 1973proved that the country had the tenacity to succeed, resulting in a greater standard of living for the population in general and the farming community in particular.

Carmel Byrne, Lil Nugent, Vincent Byrne and Una Byrne at the Gyves threashing in 1942.

These rapid developments had a profound effect on the social fabric of the Blessington community. The typical village spirit of togetherness was starting to wane, but was being replaced by a greater affluence, which was very welcome.

Greater changes were to emerge, which were to impact beneficially on the farming community in close proximity to the village. This change was driven by the industrial revolution that was taking place in tandem with the agricultural advances.

Returning immigrants, required for the industrial jobs, created an unprecedented demand for houses, and the overspill from Dublin City led to a demand for building land in Blessington. The local farmers were in the right place at the right time.

The Doran and Gyves farms and the Flanagan and Darker lands, north of the village, were acquired by Roadstone to service the building material requirement of the building boom. Eager's farm, to the west, was acquired by the County Council for local authority housing. O'Leary farm, also on the western edge of the village, is now being developed as a housing estate and new shopping centre. The Henry, Coughlan, Boothman and Millar farms to the south of the village have also been acquired for housing development.

In a relatively short number of years the vast tract of land known as Blessington Demesne, originally developed by Archbishop Boyle as prime agricultural farmland, has passed from the farming community into the hands of housing developers. Coupled with the acquisition of the farmland to the east of the village by the ESB, for the creation of Blessington lakes, these developments have completed a major change of landscape in the 20th Century.

Blessington has ceased to have an involvement in agriculture and is now a dormer town for Dublin city, but thanks for the memories.

Legend of the Public House trade, "Luv" Mullaly, his Wife and Son, Paddy.

Fair Day in Blessington, circa 1900.

Religious Denominations

THE Spiritual needs of the Blessington population were provided by the two main Christian Churches, namely the Protestant and Roman Catholic Faiths.

The main church buildings to service these communities emerged from the creation of the town itself. St. Mary's Protestant Church in 1683 and the Roman Catholic Church, The Church of Our Mother of Mercy in 1811, at Cross Chapel. It would appear there was a small church on the Cross Chapel site prior to 1811 and also at Burgage and near Woodend.

When the Celts arrived in Ireland they were a pagan race. By the fifth century they had established themselves as an embryonic Irish race. It was about this time that the Pope sent his first Bishop to Ireland and was quite successful in his endeavours to establish Christianity. St. Patrick followed and is credited with the achievement of the country's conversion.

After the reformation and the adoption of Protestantism by Henry VIII, Ireland was planted by his followers in the early 16th century. The British establishment introduced the draconian penal laws which denied the native Catholics of the right to own land, the right to an education, the right to vote, the right participate in business or the right to practice their religion. This oppression was state driven and not by the Protestant Church. Religion and education were driven "underground" and hedge schools and Mass Rocks appeared in the area.

In the case of Blessington, while the landlords were of the Protestant Faith, they were fair to their Catholic tenants within the laws under which they operated. There are many cases of benevolence by the Protestant community to the Catholic Church. The allocation of land at Cross Chapel by the Downshire Estate and the donation of stained glass windows for the Catholic Church in 1811 is a case in point.

The first rector of St Mary's Church was John Tyndall. He was followed by William Walsh Senior who was succeeded by his son William Walsh Junior. Then came Hill Benson in the 1798 period. Thomas Tucker in 1824 and Isaac Corry served before the appointment of William Moore in 1833. His estate was in Manor Kilbride and was a big landowner. He was succeeded by Samuel Meyrick. Thomas Edwards served in the 1894 period. William Scully, John Crooks, Joseph Blackwell, Eric Despard, Reginald Lowe, Richard Stokes and Nigel Dunne served with distinction in the 1900's. The Church was well

Church of Our Lady of the Most Holy Sacrament.

Interior of Churcd of The Most Holy Sacrament.

supported by parishioners such as the Horniges, the Smiths, the Leesons and Lord Downshire. The Rev. Kesh Rico Goven from Peel, takes over the parish in February 2004.

The Roman Catholic clergy included Fr.Roger Miley in 1771, Miles Miley in 1801, Michael Donellan in 1809. In 1824 Michael Toole was the incumbent and was succeeded by Francis Archer. Thomas Curran led the parish into the twentieth century with Fr. O'Carroll. Francis Maguire served during the troubled times of the 1920's, followed by Fr. Nolan, Fr. O'Keeffe with curate Fr. Lillis. Joseph Union took over until his promotion to Terenure parish and was followed by Daniel Lucey in 1953. He was appointed Parish Priest of Glasthule in 1960. He was a native of Macroom in Cork. Born in 1895, studied for the priesthood in Maynooth College and was ordained in 1919 He was a nephew of the famous Bishop Lucey of the Cork dioceses. When he moved on to Glasthule parish after an eventful stewardship in Blessington, Fr. Crinnion took over as Parish Priest followed by Fr. Casey. Fr. Lyons is now Parish Priest for the R.C. community with Fr. Tim Murphy CC.

Education in Blessington was conducted on denominational lines. The Protestant school got an early start. At the beginning of the 19th century the Marquis of Downshire was operating two schools, one for boys and one for girls. Teachers who served there were John Hamilton, Miss Grinden, John Greer and Mrs. Ruby Taylor.

The two communities lived in great harmony, even during the religious persecution perpetrated by the British establishment, and the opposition to that same establishment in 1798 and 1916. There was an air of mutual respect and support. The development of the town can be attributed to the joint and equally important contribution of the two traditions.

The British Monarchy had introduced penal laws as applicable to Ireland in the 15th 16th and 17th centuries. The legislation that they passed was designed to harass the Catholic clergy and to suppress the education of Catholic children. This gave rise to the practice of their faith at Mass Rocks and education in Hedge Schools.

The first Catholic school was planned in 1880 and was completed shortly after. Maurice Landers was principal. Mrs. Lilly O'Donnell also taught there and transferred to the new school. Maurice Landers was succeeded by James Quinn who was principal of the new school which was built in 1936. Other teachers in the school were Miss McNicholls, Miss Lavin, Miss Quinn and Miss Nuala Keeley. Miss Keeley was a strict teacher and developed the creative talents of her pupils. Her production of the school pantomime, "Snow White and The Seven Dwarfs", and a drill display team, was an occasion, which is remembered by the participants with some pride and a lot of tribulation.

Interior of St. Mary's Church.

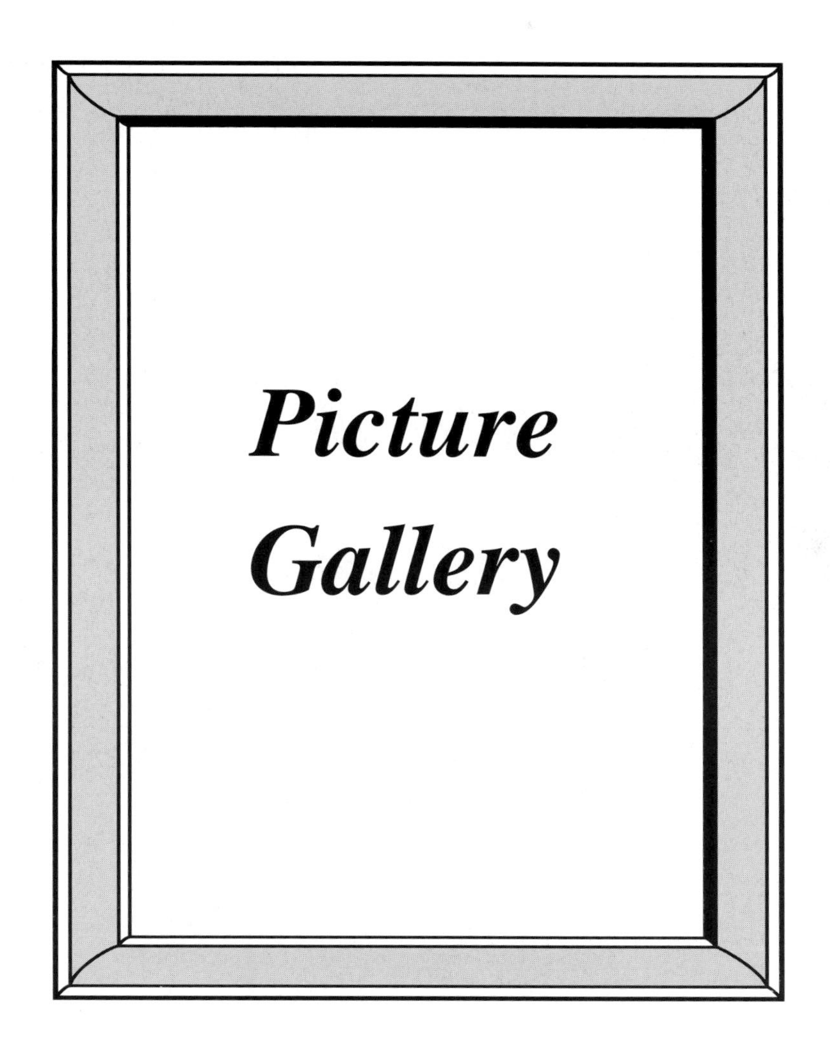
Picture
Gallery

Blessington Parish Church, Cross Chapel.

Interior of Blessington Parish Church, Cross Chapel.

Corpus Christi Procession in 1950's.

The remnants of the ruins of the old church at Woodend.
Inset: Surviving picture from the church.

Archbishop McQuaid accompanied by Fr. Joseph Union consecrates the Church of the Most Holy Sacrament Blessington on the 30th May 1946. This event enjoyed cross community involvement with the LDF commanded on the day by William Boothman, and the mounted Guard of Honour under the leadership of Jack Kane. Also in the photo are Ned Harte, Odey Tyrell Tom Tyrell and Philly Creighton. The Church was replaced by the new Church of Our Lady of the Most Holy Sacrament in 1982. which was 100 years after the structure was built as a School in 1882.

LDF Church Parade.

Blessington Fashions in 1920s

Elizabeth Moore.

Mrs. Phillips and Alice Lynch.

The Owens sisters.

Mary Moore.

Edward Moore's marriage to Kate Clarke.

"Day Out" … Lar Moore and Martin McDonald at Poulaphouca waterfall.

Boys School 1921

***Front row:** Jim Hayden, Tom Landers, John Slattery, Eoin Fitzsimons, Kevin Chambers, Bernard Hanlon, Paddy Brophy, Jim Clarke.*

***2nd row:** Bill Devoy, Paddy Redmond, Eddie Byrne, Ned Devoy, Johnny Byrne, Isaac Hamilton, John Murphy.*

***3rd row:** Martin Murphy, Pat Hanlon, Tom Clarke, Charlie Doran, Frank Murphy, Odie Tyrell, Charlie Keogh, Jim Hamilton, Jackie Brophy.*

***4th row:** Sam Kelly, Carbery Healy, Jim Nolan, Philly Creighton, Willy Doran, Tom Doran, Johnny Keogh, Barney Flanagan, Maurice Landers (Teacher)*

***Back Row:** Ned Devoy, Martin Murphy, Maurice O'Connor, Jack Murray, Bernard Hanlon.*

Boys School 1925

***Front row:** Jack Tyrell, Jack Ardagh, Tom Landers, Dickie Dowling, Pat Hanlon, Pa Tyrell.*

***2nd row.** Johnny Byrne, Paddy Flanagan, Maurice Landers.*

***Back Row:** Ned Devoy, Martin Murphy, Maurice O'Connor, Jack Murray, Bernard Hanlon.*

Drill Display Team who performed In St. Joseph's Hall on 14th January 1950.
Front row: Gabriel Murphy, Manus O'Donnell, John Brennan.
Back row: Noel Hession, Vincent Byrne, John McGrath, Brendan Byrne, Sean O'Toole.

"Snow Sculpture" of Strongbow's grave during the Big Snow of 1947.

Boys School

***Front Row.** Dickie Dowling, Pat Hanlon, Jack Tyrell (forge), Andy Hayden, Tommy White, George Devoy, Tom Landers, Tommy Fitzpatrick. Christy Clarke.*

***2nd row.** Jack Tyrell, Johnny Byrne, Jim Clarke, John Nolan, Bill Devoy, John Hayden, Jim Browne, Paddy Brophy, Bernard Hanlon, Peter Nolan, Jack Ardagh, Jack Murray, Pa Tyrell.*

***3rd row.** Dinny Doran, Pa Brophy, Jimmy Wallace, Sam Brophy, Tom Flanagan, Hugh Hamilton, John Keogh, Philly Creighton, Pa Kelly, Maurice O'Connor, Willy Doran, Ned Harte, Jim Nolan.*

***Back row.** Ned Devoy, Jimmy Keogh, Jimmy Carroll, Isaac Hamilton, Johnny Byrne, Tom Clarke, Ned Moore, Paddy Redmond, Jim Hamilton, Ned Byrne, Mick Tyrell. Christy Denison. Teachers, Lilly Hartney, (O'Donnell), Maurice Landers.*

Church of Ireland School, built by Lord Downshire.

Blessington 1974 Wicklow County Junior Champions
Back row: Pat Quinn, Arthur Hennessy, John Coogan, Des Kennedy, Martin Hennessy, Paddy Sargent, Mick Doran, Shay Sargent, Tommy Cullen, Peter Finnegan.
Front row: John Finnegan, Seamus Breen, Gerry Hennessy, Patsy Finnegan, Andy Doran, Christy Nolan, Davy Byrne, Patsy Donoghue.

Annual Dinner Dance
Front row: Jim O'Keefe, Toddy Hennessy, Fr Casey, John Coogan, Canon Lowe.
Row 2: Jimmy Hughes, Jim Halligan, Gerry Hennessy, Tommy Murphy, Michael Sargent.
Row 3: Martin Hennessy, Paddy McGee, Sean Casey, Pete Nolan, Peter Finnegan.
Back row: Odey Flannagan, Arthur Hennessy, Jack Boothman.

Annual Dinner Dance 1970-71
Back row: Paddy McGee, Pete Nolan, Peter Finnegan, Toddy Hennessy, Billy Hamilton, Bill Walshe (Club Chairman).
Front row: Arthur Hennessy, Fr Casey (Club President), "Sam Maguire" (Guest of Honour), Aidan Cruise (Secretary), Jimmy Hughes.

Annual Dinner Dance 1979
Front row: Gerry McIntyre, Odey Flanagan, Rene Hennessy, John Coogan, Gene Walsh, Pete Nolan, John Finnegan.
Row 2: Tommy Murphy, Martin Shannon, Jim Twomey, Frank Flanagan, Toddy Hennessy.
Back row: Christy Sargent, Paddy McGee, Arthur Hennessy, Shea Sargent, Frank Byrne, Michael Sargent.

Top: Frank O'Toole (Senior). Second player from left in back row on the Kildare All Ireland winning team of 1927 and 1928.

Below: Frank O'Toole (Junior). Back row, 5th from left on the Wicklow Senior team that competed in the 1956 Leinster Championship.

Flanagan homestead at Dillonstown.

Memorial to mark the site of 1941 air crash.

Dublin Metropolitan Regatta on Blessington Lake.

Eight seconds of glory – the Tour de France passes through Blessington (1998).

Hi-tec drilling equipment operating in Blessington in 1937 in preparation for the construction of the new bridge.

The John Lynch horse stables situated on the Green.

1940s threshing machine.

Horse drawn buck rake.

Horse drawn mowing machine.

The Wall family burial plot in Burgage cemetery.

Grave stone moved from old graveyard to new cemetery prior to flooding of Blessington Lake.

Three Castles, scene of the Kellway slaying.

William Gyves

Jim Clarke, Senior

Frank O'Toole, Senior

Councillor Jimmy Miley

Honora Gore, daughter of Downshire Agent James Gore who married James Moor of Burgage. She was mother of Edward, Elizabeth, Lar, and John Moore.

Blessington by night.

Paddy McGee

Pete "The Manager" Nolan

Peter Finnegan

Gerry McIntyre

Fr. Çasey, Parish Priest.

Canon Lowe, Rector.

St. Mark's Cross, transferred from old graveyard to new Burgage Cemetery prior to the flooding of Blessington Lake.

Conclusion

BLESSINGTON has come a long way since God made the World. It is now at the start of the 21st century and is in a strong position to take advantage of new technologies and to build on the experience and achievements of past generations.

The history of Blessington. is a chequered one and is fairly typical of the development of the rest of Ireland. It was lucky that it did not experience the excesses of domination and suppression that was commonplace in most of the country. The building on the talents and ingenuity of its people to consolidate past gains was inspirational and could not have been achieved without the cohesion and unity of the community as a whole. The survival instinct of the people, which was developed over the formative years, is a legacy which will greatly benefit future generations in their quest for the perfect world.

One cant help wondering what the old generation would think of the town as it is today, the Miller family traded in Blessington since the 1890's. What would Stanley Millar think of his premises being called "Brunch and Munch". John Cruise would wonder at his open front butchers shop now being called "The Goggle Box". Johnny Byrne's now bearing the grandiose title of "The Tudor Inn", and the appearance on the main street of an Italian Chipper, a Chinese Restaurant, a Pizza Parlour and Fred's Fashions. How would Archbishop Boyle view his community hall being used for "belly dancing"? As the old joke goes, "If they were alive to-day the would turn in their graves".

The future belongs to the young people and there is no doubt that they will make a good job of the challenge. In doing so they will be making the history of to-morrow.

Historical Notes